Fit for GOLF

**A Personalized Conditioning
Routine to Help You Improve Your
Score, Hit the Ball Farther, and
Enjoy the Game More**

Fit for GOLF

Boris Kuzmic
with Jim Gorant

McGraw·Hill

New York   Chicago   San Francisco   Lisbon   London   Madrid   Mexico City
Milan   New Delhi   San Juan   Seoul   Singapore   Sydney   Toronto

The **McGraw-Hill** Companies

Library of Congress Cataloging-in-Publication Data

Kuzmic, Boris.
    Fit for golf : a personalized conditioning routine to help you improve
your score, hit the ball farther, and enjoy the game more / Boris Kuzmic
with Jim Gorant.—1st ed.
        p.   cm.
    ISBN 0-07-141790-7
    1. Golf—Training.   2. Physical fitness.   I. Gorant, Jim.   II. Title.

GV979.T68 K89   2004
613.7'11—dc22   2003022643

The Jesper Parnevik interview on pages 27–28 is an outtake of an interview conducted in June 2000 as part of a story that ran in *Maximum Golf* magazine.

2 3 4 5 6 7 8 9 0   AGM/AGM   3 2 1 0 9 8 7 6 5 4

ISBN 0-07-141790-7

All exercise photos by Crawford Morgan
Model for exercise photos: Eric Duncan
Exercise photos taken at Aspen East Health Club, Upper Montclair, New Jersey
Interior design by Think Design Group

McGraw-Hill books are available at special quantity discounts to use as premiums and sales promotions, or for use in corporate training programs. For more information, please write to the Director of Special Sales, Professional Publishing, McGraw-Hill, Two Penn Plaza, New York, NY 10121-2298. Or contact your local bookstore.

In view of the complex, individual, and specific nature of health and fitness problems, this book and the ideas, programs, procedures, and suggestions in it are not intended to replace the advice of trained medical professionals. All matters regarding one's health require medical supervision. A physician should be consulted prior to adopting any program described in the book if the reader has any condition that may require diagnosis or medical attention. The authors and publisher disclaim any liability arising directly or indirectly from the use of this book.

This book is printed on acid-free paper.

Contents

Foreword

Several years ago someone told me that once you hit thirty-five you have to work harder just to keep playing golf at the same level. I want to play until I'm fifty-five, and I don't want to be one of those guys just barely clinging to the PGA Tour. I want to keep getting better and I want to win.

So when I turned thirty-five, I hired Boris Kuzmic as my personal trainer and started working out. I liked Boris's background as both a professional golfer and fitness expert, and with the workout plan he designed for me, my torso strength and flexibility improved and my clubhead speed increased, which allowed me to hit the ball farther.

Before long, working out became such a part of my routine that I regarded it as essential as hitting balls and practicing putting. I built a gym in my house and put a stair-climber in the TV room. Most people don't know this, but on the final Sunday of the 2000 Masters I had to go out early to finish my third round before playing the final round. Boris and I met at 5:45 A.M. to spend a half hour in the gym getting warm and loose. I played twenty-two holes that day and wound up winning the tournament, which gives you some idea of how important fitness had become to me and my game.

That's an extreme situation, but whether you're a weekend golfer, an aspiring junior player, or just someone who's trying to get better, working out can help you, too. You can't hire Boris, like I did, but he has put everything he knows about exercise for golfers into this book, which is almost sure to help.

Although Boris has moved back to Sweden, I continue to work out harder than ever and I never miss a day. In fact, when I'm at home I often work out twice a day—in the morning before practice and then again afterward. Last year, at the age of forty, I won four times on the PGA Tour, recorded eighteen top ten finishes, and ended up first on the money list, so I think it's safe to say that adding physical fitness to my golf routine has certainly worked out for me. I'm sure it can help you, too.

Vijay Singh

Acknowledgments

I'd like to thank my entire family and my friends, and especially Lena Holmberg for having the patience and faith in me to give up her job and spend two years traveling on the PGA Tour when neither of us really knew what would come of it. I'd also like to thank all my clients who made my time on the Tour such a good experience. I'd especially like to thank the Hjertstedt family and the Singh family for their hospitality. And last I'd like to thank Jim Gorant for making this book happen.

Boris Kuzmic

I wish to thank everyone at McGraw-Hill Trade; my mentors/friends in the magazine world—Carolyn Kitch, Richard Thiel, Maura Fritz, Mark Adams, and Joe Bargmann, as well as Craig Peden, Evan Rothman, and Michael Verdon; My Big Fat Greek Miracle Worker, Jimmy (Tyler?) Pappas; the photographer with the reversed name, Crawford Morgan; and next year's "it" boy, Eric Duncan. From the "there wouldn't be a book without them" category: the most relaxed busy man in the universe, Boris Kuzmic; my parents, George and Lucy, for the love and support; and for all the things that I don't think I will ever find words for, the lovely and beautiful Karin Anne Henderson.

Jim Gorant

Fit for
GOLF

What to Expect

Ever since Tiger Woods exploded onto the golf scene and attributed part of his success to daily workouts, physical fitness has become one of the fastest-growing areas of interest for golfers. Tiger worked out hard, even on the days he played. This was unheard of on the PGA Tour.

Before Tiger, a few golfers did pay attention to physical fitness—most notably Gary Player—but most of them weren't consistent and didn't really do the kind of work that would make a difference in their play. Two and half years later, after Tiger had conquered the golf world, the workout facilities at every PGA stop were jammed with players every day. These guys suddenly realized that if they wanted to keep up with the best they could no longer focus solely on swing planes and putting strokes.

The same is true for the rest of us: to play better golf, we need to improve every aspect of our games and our bodies. I'm a former professional golfer who went on to become the personal trainer for eleven PGA Tour players—David Duval, Ernie Els, Vijay Singh, Jesper Parnevik, Robert Allenby, Tom Pernice Jr., Gabriel Hjertstedt, Gary Nicklaus,

Tiger Woods (Photo by Darren Carroll/DCfoto)

Tommy Armour, Brad Fabel, and Tim Herron. While working with me, five of them were ranked among the top twenty golfers in the world.

Although working out is great for the pros, it may do even more for the amateur golfer. By following a well-designed fitness and nutrition program like the ones in this book, you can expect to:

- hit the ball farther
- gain control over your swing
- improve your flexibility and range of motion
- increase your stamina

Before Working Out and After Working Out

Before working out with me, David Duval weighed 220 pounds and had a 38-inch waist. Afterward, he weighed 186 pounds and had a 32-inch waist. Here are a few other numbers that demonstrate the difference between life before and after training with me:

	Before	After
David Duval		
Majors	0	2001 British Open
Average drive	1996: 274 yards	2001: 294 yards
Vijay Singh		
Majors	0	1998 PGA, 2000 Masters
All-around rank	1998: 31	2003: 2
Jesper Parnevik		
Tour wins	0	5
Average drive	1998: 266 yards	2003: 281 yards
All-around rank	1998: 88	2000: 28
Robert Allenby		
Tour wins	0	4
Top tens	2	23
Ernie Els		
Average drive	1998: 271 yards	2003: 304 yards
All-around rank	1998: 55	2000: 5
Tom Pernice Jr.		
Tour wins	0	2
Top tens	1	11
Gabe Hjertstedt		
Average drive	1997: 267 yards	2003: 280 yards
All-around rank	1998: 175	2000: 109

Source: PGATour.com

- lose weight
- minimize your risk of injury
- decrease postround muscle soreness
- gain self-confidence
- improve your overall level of fitness and health (reducing the risk of heart disease, diabetes, certain types of cancer, and high blood

pressure; strengthening the immune system; increasing longevity and energy; and creating better overall strength, coordination, and balance)

But what about the scorecard, you're wondering? *How much better can I expect to get by spending some time in the gym?* Well, expectations are always tough to quantify. Everyone's different. Golfers swing differently, they have different problems, and their bodies react differently to physical exertion. That doesn't mean I won't give you some hard numbers, though, because goals will help you start and stick to a routine. While you're lying in bed thinking that you don't want to work out today, having a concrete number in your head might help get you out from under the covers. If you can tell yourself, *Get up and run and stretch and lift—if you do, you can drop five shots off your score*, that's pretty good inspiration.

And that's about right, too. Based on my experience, the average 15- to 20-handicap player can shave as many as four to six shots by regularly following a workout plan like the ones prescribed in these pages. That's not a guarantee or a promise, but it's an estimation based on years of watching people use the gym to improve their play.

One story that comes to mind involves a friend back in Sweden who took up the game relatively late in life, in his late twenties. He had been a member of the Swedish national badminton team, so he was a good athlete with exceptional hand-eye coordination. In addition, he considered himself to be in pretty good shape, certainly good enough to play golf. However, after two years his handicap lingered at 28 and he grew ever more frustrated with the game.

Gary Player (Photo courtesy of The Player Group)

Finally, he agreed to let me design a golf-specific workout plan for him. Within one year, his handicap was down to 15.

That's a dramatic improvement—the most dramatic I can think of—and although it will not be everyone's experience, it does hint at the possibilities. At the same time, I've seen people take on a full workout regimen without noticing any difference on their scorecard, and that's certainly a possibility as well. But that doesn't mean there wasn't a difference in their golf game.

Gabe Hjertstedt Talks About Golf, Boris, and Working Out

Q: What has working with Boris meant to your career?

GH: I hated working out, and one of the big things I got from Boris was a lot of positive thinking along with the weightlifting. And that changed a lot about my golf game. As I got stronger, I felt better on the golf course and I started to hit the ball farther. It made a big impact on me.

Q: Are you hitting it farther?

GH: Yeah, 10 to 15 yards with the driver. But all in all I'm a better person. I feel better about myself.

Q: Because?

GH: When I started with Boris I had a lot of negative thoughts, and Boris had a way of getting rid of those. We had a lot of fun. If you enjoy yourself when you're doing something, that always shows in the results. It was sometimes hard to get up in the morning. When we had a 7:30 tee time, we usually started warming up three hours beforehand, so we'd have to get up at 4:30 in the morning and go to the gym and ride the bike and whatever else. So unless you have someone knocking on your door, it's easy to skip. So the initial few months it helps to have that outside motivation, but eventually you get to the stage where you want to do it and you know it's part of your routine.

Q: It's more than just weight training, then?

GH: It was a lot of good fun and good camaraderie combined with physical training and good mental focus. I think the mind is a huge thing and I know now that the physical part is a very big part of the mental side. Hand-in-hand, as they say.

Q: Did you even work out on the days of tournaments?

GH: Yeah, we would try. I mean, I think I was probably one of the guinea pigs on that. We did. And we experimented a little. Some mornings we'd do just an upper-body workout or whatever. You get to a stage where as long as you finish three hours before your tee time it's not going to affect you in any way. You might even feel a bit jacked up from it.

Q: Will you ever go back to not working out?

GH: No. For me to be competitive, I've got to stay on a really strict program. It might be different if I were 6'1" or 6'2"—you know, a lot of people are big naturally, but I'm not, so I have to really work out to keep up, which I'm able to do.

Q: Did it affect your flexibility?

GH: No. I was able to get more flexible even as I was getting stronger.

Q: Did you have doubts at the beginning?

GH: Not really. No one really told me, but I knew I wasn't strong. Sometimes you think you're strong but you're not. I used to play in these charity events with athletes from other sports, and these guys may not have the best technique but they could still hit it out there 310 or 320 yards. That's because they had that core strength and the leg strength. So I always knew that if you had those things you were going to be able to whip it out there pretty good.

Q: How big has working out on the Tour become?

GH: We were some of the first ones to do it. Tiger obviously was working out, but there was really no one who traveled with a personal trainer. Now you look and there are a bunch of guys doing it. You get some players who still don't work out that much, and I think they're going to suffer down the road when the one side is so much stronger than the other. You need that balance and that pure strength you get from weightlifting. Golf is an explosion sport. Some people say it's not, but it is, and players are only going to get bigger and stronger.

Born in Umea, Sweden, in 1971, Gabe Hjertstedt turned pro at the age of eighteen and played on the Australian, Japanese, and European tours before qualifying for the U.S. Tour in 1996. In 1997 he became the first Swede to win on the Tour by capturing the B.C. Open, which he followed by winning the Touchstone Energy Tucson Classic in 1999.

Gabe Hjertstedt
(Photo courtesy of Ping Golf)

Working out can enhance your game and life in so many ways beyond just knocking a few shots off your score. On the golf course it will increase your strength, flexibility, stamina, and energy. You'll be able to make a bigger turn and get to a better finish while feeling more balanced throughout the swing. And you'll not only hit the ball harder with less effort, but you'll still feel fresh as you approach the end of your round and have reserves of power and control necessary to pull off any kind of shot when it counts most.

In addition, working out will help build that ever-elusive *muscle memory*, the process in which your body learns through repetition to refine and repeat a certain movement. This is how great golfers build such consistent swings, by ingraining the motion into their muscles so that when the time comes they don't have to think about it—the body just does it the right way. Being in better shape gives you more control over your muscles and enhances your ability to groove your swing through practice.

Off the course, regular workouts can lower your risk of heart disease, aid in weight loss, bolster your immune system, and relieve stress. That same feeling of increased stamina and energy that can help lower your score will also make you feel better in everything you do, whether that's sitting through marathon four-hour meetings at the office or mowing

Vijay Singh (Photo courtesy of Cleveland Golf)

the lawn. You'll have that same sense of doing more with less effort, which makes everything more enjoyable.

Working out can do wonders for your state of mind as well. As you start to feel stronger and lose weight, you'll feel better about yourself, more confident. Golf is a game of confidence, and the boost in self-esteem you'll get from being in better physical condition will make you more assured in everything you do, both on and off the course.

In addition, a well-trained body is less likely to suffer injuries and more likely to recover from them quickly. In fact, it's lack of flexibility and your body's attempts to compensate for muscle weaknesses and imbalances that cause many injuries in the first place.

What else can you expect? Well, expect to do some work. Depending on your goals and your current condition, you're looking at an hourlong workout three to five days a week. I firmly believe that workouts shouldn't last more than sixty minutes—including stretching, cardiovascular conditioning, and weight training. At the beginning, almost everyone will start with a three-day program and build up to five days. After that, workouts should increase in intensity and frequency instead of duration.

How do I know all this? As a teenager growing up in my native Sweden, I played my way into the national program for promising young golfers. As a part of that program I took part in tournaments throughout Europe alongside some of the best players in my country, including

Robert Karlson, Pierre Fulke, Joakim Haeggman, and Claus Eriksen, all of whom are successful players on the European PGA Tour today.

I always figured I'd be out there with them, especially when at eighteen I became the assistant pro at Emmaboda, my hometown course. I was working with a renowned swing guru named Farid Guedra, who also tutored another promising young pro who had already won the Malaysian Open and the Nigerian Open. His name was Vijay Singh. Of course, Vijay would go on to become one of the best players in the game. As Vijay and I became friends, often practicing and playing together at the club, I felt I had just as good a chance to break out from the pack as he did.

In fact, before Vijay's explosion onto the European Tour, I landed a sponsorship deal and headed to Miami to spend the winter working on my game and playing in the mini-tours. When that sponsorship ceased, I played my way into a second one and kept right on going. There was just one problem. For several weeks I'd had pain in my left ankle. It turned out that I had a bone spur that had become so swollen and infected that I could barely put on a shoe and I walked with a severe limp. Before I knew it, I was back in Sweden having surgery.

Two weeks after that I was back on the golf course, but the ankle problems returned and I ended up having two more surgeries over the next six months. Faced with the probable end of my competitive playing days, I tried to figure out what went wrong.

I'd been working out for as long as I'd been playing golf and had always held a deep curiosity about physical fitness and the human body. I asked a lot of questions, but no one could explain what had happened and why it had gotten so bad. I decided to investigate.

At the Scandinavian Academy of Fitness Education, I signed up for a three-week course designed to teach the basics of physiology and biomechanics and provide a personal training certification. It was interesting but didn't come close to answering my questions. I returned to the academy for five longer, in-depth levels of personal training school, at the end of which I received a worldwide certification as a personal trainer. To round out this education, I attended Manumetic, a Swedish massage school. When it was all said and done, I was twenty-two years old and still didn't have any answers about my ankle, but I had found a new career.

I took a job as the head instructor for rehab, personal training, and massage at the largest treatment center in the city, Stockholm Chiropractic Clinic. Over the next six years I maintained a stable of forty to fifty clients and treated every condition imaginable. It was as if I had spent most of my teens learning everything I could about golf, and now I was spending my twenties learning everything I could about physical fitness, personal training, and the workings of the human body. Then suddenly, unexpectedly, the two bodies of knowledge came together.

Shortly before the 1998 Scandinavian Masters, I got a call from an old friend who knew Gabriel Hjertstedt, a local hero and the first Swedish golfer ever to win an event on the U.S. Tour. Gabe was in town for a few weeks to play the Masters, but he was having a problem with his calf and the friend wondered if I could help.

I met with Gabe the next day, examined his leg, and put him through a series of strength and conditioning tests. I discovered that Gabe had been playing with a severe tear of his calf muscle and that he was dreadfully weak and out of shape. I put together a program to rehab the leg and improve Gabe's strength and conditioning. By the time he was ready to return to the States, Gabe was so convinced that the workout regimen I had designed would improve his game that he didn't want to quit. What would happen when he returned to the ten-month grind of weekly travel, hotel food, and long plane rides that is the PGA Tour? He wanted me to come back with him for a few weeks and get him started on a program he could maintain while playing and traveling.

So I headed to the United States with Gabe. Within a few days of arriving I ran into my old friend Vijay, who was flirting with a permanent place among the top players in the game. Like many other golfers, Vijay had come to see better physical conditioning as one last area of improvement that could push him over the top. Tiger Woods had not yet set the Tour on fire, but he had already provided an example of the younger, stronger, more athletic golfer making his way into the pro game. About a year earlier, Vijay had started working out casually in his home with his wife's personal trainer, but he was interested in doing something more consistent, focused, and golf specific. Within days I was working with him as well.

Initially the three of us—Vijay, Gabe, and I—attracted a lot of side-long glances in the gym. We were doing things that few (if any) players had seen before. But that was just idle curiosity. What really drew the interest of other players was Vijay's and Gabe's improved play. Vijay started playing the best golf of his career and became a fixture on the weekly leaderboard and in the top ten world rankings, capped by his wins at the 1998 PGA and 2000 Masters. Gabe, who had always been one of the shortest hitters on the Tour, suddenly started hitting the ball farther, even ranking third in driving distance at the 1999 Vegas Open.

Word spread. Players could see the value of working with someone who was not only a physical fitness expert but who understood the game and what it took to play at a high level with regularity. Within six months of arriving in the States, I had eleven full-time clients and ten more on a waiting list. I had finally made it on the PGA Tour.

In the following chapters, I'll share with you the techniques I used while training those PGA players. We'll start with my basic philosophy of working out, and then I'll show you a system by which you can evaluate your own body's strengths and weaknesses. With that knowledge you can move on to the carefully explained and photographed exercises to design a workout that works specifically for your needs. The chapter following that one will offer a number of sample workout programs that are designed to fit different needs and schedules. To round things out, we'll work through a few chapters on nutrition, injuries, special groups of golfers (juniors and seniors), the mental side of the game, and, best of all, what to do if you really want to hit it far.

I hope this book inspires you to start on a regular fitness regimen and makes you a better golfer as well as a healthier person.

The Key Goal of Working Out

If you pick up another golf fitness book or stop by a local gym where they offer a golf-training program, you'll probably see and hear the term *golf muscles* thrown around. Everybody's always going on about the training that's going to develop your specific "golf muscles," by which they often mean the rotator cuff muscles of your shoulders, the spine stabilization muscles of your middle and lower back, and the transverse muscles of your abdomen and hips, often referred to as the *core muscles*. But when you ask those same people to tell you which muscles are involved in a good golf swing, they'll give you a list that includes every major muscle group from the neck to the calves. So, what's the deal?

One of the things that makes golf so difficult is that it requires you to use your entire body to perform a very precise task. It's something like trying to write your name on the ground with a pencil held in your belly button. Although the swing obviously involves many muscles, exactly which ones play what part has been a matter of debate in the past. But various researchers using electromyography (EMG), a process that determines muscle activity by tracing electrical impulses, have uncovered surprising answers to those questions.

As expected, they learned that the golf swing requires the highly coordinated activation of almost every major muscle group in the body, and that many of the logical suspects play a big part—the legs, hips, back, and abdominals. What surprised some was how big a role the pecs (chest muscles) of the trailing side played, how much the lats (outer back muscles) dominated throughout the swing, and how little the delts (the major shoulder muscles) did. Instead, the rotator cuff muscles inside the shoulder have a much bigger part in the swing.

Following is a list of all the muscles that come into play in the golf swing. The steady, balanced development of all of them—not just the oft-cited "golf muscles"—will help make you a better golfer.

- Quadriceps (front thigh)
- Hamstrings (back thigh)
- Abductors (hips)
- Adductors (inside thigh)
- Glutes (buttocks)
- Obliques (outer torso)
- Erectors (lower back)
- Latissimus dorsi, rhomboids, trapezius (middle and upper back)
- Pectorals (chest)
- Deltoids (shoulder)
- Infraspinatus, teres minor, subscapularis, supraspinatus (rotator cuff)
- Triceps (back upper arm)
- Biceps (front upper arm)
- Forearm flexors and extensors (forearm)

The truth is that these "golf muscles" are crucial to the swing, but no more crucial than any of the other muscles are. It's just that those particular muscles are less frequently used and often underdeveloped, so they offer an easy and obvious target for anyone trying to sell a golf workout program. Certainly, those muscles do need to be developed—and I have some specific methods to do that—but so do almost all the rest of the muscles in your body. The ultimate goal should be *muscle balance*, a key to enhanced performance and reduced injuries in almost any athletic endeavor.

On the simplest level, muscle balance means that your left arm isn't any stronger than your right arm and vice versa. This is very important in golf, where you're supposed to control and deliver about 80 percent of your power with the nondominant side of your body. That's hard for anyone to do, but even harder if your dominant side is twice as strong as the nondominant side.

On a deeper level, muscle balance is about an overall equilibrium of strength and flexibility between the opposing muscles of your body. Fitness experts like to compare muscle imbalance to a car with improper alignment. The car looks fine, but over time the imbalance begins to affect performance. The tires wear unevenly. The car pulls to one side and generally doesn't handle the way it should. There's extra stress on the steering system and axles and suspension that can lead to bigger problems down the road.

Likewise, your body gets out of alignment and needs to be adjusted. Each joint in the body—even the vertebrae—is surrounded and supported by muscles that allow it to move and help hold it in place. If one of those muscles gets a little stronger or weaker, or if an injury or activity stretches or tightens one element, it throws off the entire balance and causes the joint to get out of whack. It may not be noticeable to the untrained eye, but over time it can cause performance difficulties and even injury—if not to the joint itself, then to other muscles and joints that have been recruited to compensate for the original problem.

For instance, if you work at a desk typing all day, you're forced into a position where your shoulders roll forward. Over a long period of time this causes the chest muscles attached to the front of the shoulders to cramp and shorten because they are always forced into that position. Meanwhile, the muscles of your upper back, which are attached to the back of your shoulder, stretch and lengthen.

As a result, eventually you will assume a posture with your shoulders rolled forward even when you're not at the desk typing. This posture can lead to a number of conditions, from impingement syndrome to bursitis, especially when you're putting your shoulder through the extreme range of motion required for a golf swing. It's all because you have lost your muscle balance. The solution is to design a workout that will stretch the muscles of your chest that are attached to the front of your shoulders and strengthen and contract the muscles of your upper back, thereby restoring proper body alignment and putting your muscles back into balance.

The same kind of analysis can be applied to the rest of your body. Are your hamstrings too tight, preventing you from bending properly at address? You must loosen them up and strengthen the quadriceps to balance them out. Even if you can bend properly, having tight hamstrings can cause your pelvis to tilt, which sets off a chain reaction of muscular and skeletal adjustments that can put your body out of whack and set you on a collision course with injury.

To make matters worse, the golf swing itself, by no means a biomechanically efficient motion, actually *promotes* muscle imbalance. During a swing, you push off hard on your right thigh (for righties), and especially your calf, while your left leg is almost stationary. At the top it's just the opposite, with your left shoulder, hip, and back getting all the work while the right side of your chest pushes down.

If you start hitting 150 balls a week at the range in an effort to improve your game, you're going to start developing muscle imbalances based on the uneven pushing and pulling necessary for the swing. If you don't do something to counteract those imbalances, they're going to make it hard to perform at your peak level and will likely lead to some sort of injury down the road.

Moreover, proper muscle balance promotes good posture, which is a key to better, more consistent golf swings. Whether it's too much curve in your back, legs that are too straight, or a reverse tilt, how you stand both on and off the course affects how you set up over the ball, and a poor setup can decrease your chances of striking the ball solidly before you even move the club. Good muscle balance, and therefore good posture, allows you to set up in a position that gives you the best chance to hit the ball well every time and to use all your muscles within their proper range of motion. That way you'll not only hit it well, but you'll hit it far and in a way that reduces the chance of injury.

A workout that isolates and attempts to strengthen a few specific "golf muscles" might yield some short-term benefits but won't do everything possible to improve your game and could even hurt you down the road. My workout programs include elements to train those muscles through golf-specific movements (largely through the use of medicine balls), but they're just one element of an overall muscle balance regimen.

Furthermore, I believe in the benefit of pumping actual iron. You'll see a lot of golf fitness programs out there that promote low-resistance moves with surgical or elastic tubing or that focus on a lot of balance work or plyometrics, and even some yoga and Pilates takeoffs. Although all of those are valuable and can have a place in an overall workout routine, they can't replicate the muscle- and strength-building benefits of lifting weights. For the other stuff, the medicine ball throws I prescribe not only build strength and flexibility in the "golf muscles" but develop balance, coordination, and concentration. They even have a cardiovascular element.

It all feeds back into the key goal of working out—balance. Of course, in order to get started, you first have to understand your body's imbalances, which we'll discuss in the next chapter.

Your Body,
Your Workout

No two of the eleven players I've worked with on the PGA Tour have identical workouts. That's because each player has different needs, and their programs have been designed to match their individual requirements. The most effective workouts are those that are customized.

It would be nice if you could design a workout based on your swing needs. For instance, say your right side is so much stronger than your left that it dominates your swing and causes you to hit a snap hook. Then you could work to build up your left side, balancing the power and getting the hook under control. Unfortunately, there could be twenty different reasons why you're hitting that hook, so it's a question for your swing coach and not necessarily your trainer, although a workout that promotes good muscle balance, greater flexibility, and proper posture will go a long way toward solving all sorts of swing flaws.

The trick, then, is to customize a workout based on other factors. Some factors to consider include age (see Chapter 8), available time (see Chapter 7), and, most important, your body's imbalances. When I work with an individual client, I identify those imbalances and determine how to correct them by putting the client through a series of strength and flexibility tests and asking a lot of questions. For this reason, I recommend visiting a physical therapist or personal trainer in your area for a professional assessment. These professionals can not only identify your areas of need very quickly and relatively inexpensively but can also show you how to perform certain exercises that will help remedy these problem areas.

Short of that, a handful of tests and guidelines that I present in this chapter will allow you to evaluate yourself. These examinations of strength, flexibility, posture, and body type won't be as complete as a personal evaluation by a professional trainer or physical therapist, but they will allow you to make specific adjustments in your program that will better suit your individual needs. If you do think you've identified an imbalance or area of need in your own body, proceed cautiously and remember that it's always better to stretch first and regain a normal range of motion before beginning to strengthen opposed muscle groups.

Strength

Start by doing a set of push-ups. Lie facedown with your hands beside your shoulders, palms down. Contract your stomach and lower back muscles to keep your spine straight, then push yourself up until your arms are fully extended. For men, only the hands and toes should touch the floor. Women can perform a modified push-up, in which the hands and knees touch the floor. At the bottom of each repetition, your chest should come within two inches of the ground and be lower than your stomach. Do as many as you can and rate your performance using the following chart. If you fall below average, you might have to improve your upper-body strength. When choosing a workout program in Chapter 7, you should consider adding an extra set of work for the chest, arms, shoulders, and back.

Push-Ups

Age	Under 20	20–29	30–39	40–49	50–59	60–69
Men						
Good	35+	30+	25+	20+	18+	15+
Average	25–34	20–29	15–24	11–19	10–17	6–14
Poor	<25	<20	<15	<11	<10	<6
Women						
Good	25+	23+	20+	18+	15+	12+
Average	12–24	12–22	10–19	8–17	7–14	5–12
Poor	<12	<12	<10	<8	<7	<5

No matter how many push-ups you can do, take note of whether you can keep your back straight during the movement. If your belly button sags toward the floor, this signals a weakness in your mid-torso, and you should probably do an extra set of abdominal and lower back work. To further assess your torso strength, try doing the one-minute sit-up test.

Lie on your back with your knees bent, feet flat, and your arms extended in front of you. Contract your stomach and sit up until your fingers touch your knees, making sure not to pull with your head and keeping your lower back flat on the floor. See how many sit-ups you can do in sixty seconds, then use the chart on page 22 to rate your results. Again, if you fall into the "poor" category, consider some extra work for the abdominals and lower back.

Next, move on to squats. Stand with your feet slightly wider than shoulder width and your arms extended straight in front of you. Keeping your back straight, lower yourself as if you were going to sit in a chair by bending your knees (you may want to do this over a bench or low chair in case you fall). Once your upper legs are parallel with the floor, stop, and return to the starting position. Use the chart on page 22 to rate your performance. If you have a below-average score, add an extra set of work for the front and back of your thighs and your hips.

Sit-Ups

Age	Under 20	20–29	30–39	40–49	50–59	60–69
Men						
Good	40+	35+	30+	25+	20+	17+
Average	34–39	30–34	25–29	20–24	15–19	12–16
Poor	<34	<30	<25	<20	<15	<12
Women						
Good	35+	30+	24+	17+	14+	13+
Average	30–34	25–29	19–23	13–16	10–13	9–12
Poor	<30	<25	<19	<13	<10	<9

Squats

Age	Under 20	20–29	30–39	40–49	50–59	60–69
Men						
Good	40+	35+	30+	25+	20+	18+
Average	35–39	30–34	25–29	21–24	17–19	14–17
Poor	<35	<30	<25	<21	<17	<14
Women						
Good	33+	29+	25+	19+	16+	13+
Average	28–32	24–28	20–24	14–18	11–15	9–12
Poor	<28	<24	<20	<14	<11	<9

Keep in mind that the ratings are relative and that what you're looking for are inequities in your overall conditioning. If you rate "good" in push-ups and squats but "average" in sit-ups, then you should probably do extra abdominal work until that area of your body catches up to the rest. At the same time, if you rate "poor" in all three categories, then there's no need to do any extra work in any one area because all three segments of your body need to be worked on. Proceeding with a normal workout program as described in Chapter 7 should help you develop in an overall, uniform manner.

Flexibility

Good golf and solid muscle balance require flexibility, and the stretching programs outlined later in this book are designed to provide optimal range of motion through all the joints in your body. Still, golf does require stretching some body parts more than others—particularly the shoulders, back, hips, and the main structure of the torso. Therefore, it's helpful to know beforehand if you have a full range of motion in these areas. If not, you should take a few minutes to stretch them, even on days when you're not working out and right before hitting the golf course.

To test your shoulders, put your right arm straight up in the air, then bend it downward toward your back so your hand comes down behind your neck. Put your left arm at your side and bend it behind your back and up toward your right hand so that the back of your left hand presses against your back and your fingers point toward the ceiling. Try to make the fingers of your right hand and left hand touch. Switch hands and try again from the other side. If they touch or come pretty close, you have a normal range of motion; if not, work in extra repetitions of the shoulder stretches from Chapter 4.

To test your spine rotation, lie on your back with your arms straight out at your sides, knees bent at 45 degrees and feet flat on the floor. Rotate your hips and allow your legs to fall to the right until your right thigh lies flat on the floor. Repeat on the other side. If your shoulders and arms remain flat on the floor throughout, you have a normal range; if not, consider extra back stretches.

To test the sides of your back (lats), assume the same position on your back with your knees bent, but extend your arms up over your head until they lie flat on the floor, keeping your upper arms against your ears. If you can't get the arms all the way down or if you can but it pulls your lower back off the floor, then you should do some extra stretching on the sides of your back and your chest.

You can move on to the hip test without getting up. This time extend your left leg so it lies flat on the floor and keep your right knee raised. Grab your right knee with both hands and pull it toward your chest. If you can pull it so your upper leg is past perpendicular with the floor and your left leg stays flat on the ground, you have normal flexibility. If not, do extra hip stretches.

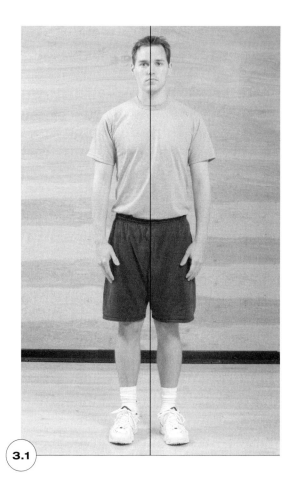

3.1

Posture

To evaluate your posture, hang a plumb line in front of a large mirror. If you don't have a large mirror, get someone to help you do this evaluation. Once the plumb line is up, stand with it centered between your feet, your ankles about three inches apart. Position either the mirror or your partner directly in front of you. The line should run directly down the center of your body (3.1). First, check the alignment of your shoulders and hips. If one shoulder or hip seems lower than the other, consult a physical therapist, as this could be a sign of a relatively serious condition such as a curved spine or a short leg.

Now look at your arms; the thumb should point forward and the first knuckle should be visible. If you can see most of the back of your hand,

3.2

you need to stretch the chest muscles and tighten the upper back and the back of the shoulders. If the thumbs point out, stretch the upper back.

Next, turn to the side and stand so the plumb line runs through the center of your hip (3.2). Check the position of your knee; the line should pass just in front of the point where the joint bends. If it hangs forward of that point and your knee seems to almost curve backward, the joint is hyperextended. You need to stretch the muscles on the front of the thigh and strengthen those in back—and stretching the tight muscle always takes precedence over strengthening the weak one. If the line hangs behind the bending point, your knee is flexed and you must stretch the back of the thigh (hamstrings) and strengthen the front of the thigh (quadriceps).

Next, check your elbows. They should be slightly bent and the line should run right through the center of the shoulder. If the shoulders roll forward, you need to stretch the chest muscles and strengthen the upper back. And don't forget the head. The line should pass right through the middle of the ear and the chin should be basically flat. If your head hangs forward, you need to stretch the chest and abdomen and strengthen the neck and upper back muscles.

An uneven or twisted stance will affect your ability to play good golf. Although there are no easy fixes, an overall stretching and strengthening routine should help.

Body Types

Three general body types exist, and knowing which type you are can help you further tweak your workouts.

Ectomorphs are the type of people who never seem to get fat—which is generally good, except that their high metabolism also makes it hard

Ernie Els (Photo courtesy of The Acushnet Company)

Tim Herron (Photo courtesy of The Acushnet Company)

for them to put on muscle. Jesper Parnevik is a prototypical ectomorph. For ectomorphs I recommend focusing more on muscle and strength building and doing less cardiovascular work.

Next up are the *mesomorphs*, people like Vijay Singh and Ernie Els, who have a thicker, medium to large build. These types are naturally stronger and can gain or lose weight relatively easily based on their activity level and diet, which is why they should maintain a steady cardio program to keep the weight off and do high reps when lifting weights so they don't get bulky.

Finally, we have the *endomorphs*, large-boned people who tend to be overweight and have a very difficult time losing weight. One great golfer I've worked with, Tim Herron, is a good example. Endomorphs should put in some extra cardiovascular time and maintain a quick pace throughout their workout to help burn calories.

Jesper Parnevik Discusses Tiger Woods and the Importance of Working Out

Q: How did you get started working out?

JP: I've always worked out, every day, even before Tiger. I've always run a lot, too, since I was young, just as a way to stay in shape and stay strong. Since Tiger came along, though, everyone's doing more and a lot of guys who never did anything are starting to do something, and it's all because of him.

Q: Why's that?

JP: He's just a little better in every aspect of the game right now. It doesn't seem like a lot, but it adds up. If you hit one more green, make one more up and down, drop one more six footer per round, over the four rounds of a tournament that adds up to twelve strokes. For a lot of guys, getting in shape and getting stronger is one way to try to close that gap.

Q: So is strength the goal?

JP: Not just strength, but if you look at the top players in the game today, they're strong guys. Vijay [Singh] and Ernie [Els] are big guys, and Duval really got big—his shoulders are so wide. And of course Tiger is massive; he's like a defensive back.

Q: For you, though, there are other considerations. True?

JP: I have an occasional heart arrhythmia, which is really nothing more than an irregular heartbeat that's brought on by fatigue and stress. Sometimes my heart rate just gets going really fast and stays like that, and I have to take some time off to let everything settle down. By working out I can increase my stamina and relieve stress, so it helps keep the arrhythmia in check.

Q: For such a small country, Sweden seems to produce an awful lot of world-class athletes—in golf, tennis, hockey, soccer, skiing. Why do you think that is?

JP: Everything here is very open and very inexpensive, and people are really encouraged to try things. Growing up I played hockey and tennis and squash and I was a really good skier, and all those sports are very popular here. I think that playing so many different things helps you find out what you're really good at, and it helps you develop as just a good overall athlete.

Born in Sweden, Jesper Parnevik has split time between his homeland and Florida since turning pro in 1988. Since then he's won nine times around the world and five times on the PGA Tour.

Jesper Parnevik
(Photo courtesy of Wilson Golf)

Beyond Home Analysis

If you never customize your workout and simply use a general exercise program like the ones I've outlined later in this book, you will probably get stronger, more flexible, and more physically fit. However, by following the guidelines in this chapter for altering your workout to best fit your body, you will get what I call a *semi-customized workout* that will help you even more by improving your posture and muscle balance.

In some cases, observing and diagnosing problems that need to be addressed is so simple that you can correct the problems using the self-analysis techniques explained in this book. Although this is helpful for most, it's still one step short of a truly customized workout program.

In many other cases, however, the tests, observations, and treatments are far from easy. For example, a trained professional would also make observations from behind to check factors such as shoulder blade position, scoliosis, and rib cage level, but these are things you can't observe on your own and that an untrained partner could not detect. In addition, there are far more detailed elements of the tests described here that determine things such as whether hip tilt is a result of overpronation, a curved spine, or just having one leg shorter than the other.

The treatments are also detailed, involving particular muscles and groups of muscles that work together. In some cases, it's not enough to say you must strengthen the hamstrings, because in reality you must strengthen the lateral hamstring while stretching the medial hamstring. Most of us wouldn't even know where to begin such an undertaking.

This is why those of you who feel you have some serious weaknesses and imbalances should consider working with, or at least consulting, a personal trainer or physical therapist before starting your exercise routine (and, as always, consult a physician, too).

Short of that, the next best thing you can do for your body and your golf game is to keep reading.

Stretching

Misconceptions and outdated information about stretching abound. For instance, most people don't realize that there are different types of flexibility and different types of stretching, that stretching can actually build strength, and that it's possible to be too flexible.

Moreover, many people may not realize that proper stretching offers a whole host of health benefits besides flexibility. It minimizes the risk of injury, cuts recovery time after injury, and helps reduce muscle soreness after activity. It also reduces muscle tension, helping you feel more relaxed, and therefore encourages a more relaxed state of mind.

Most important for golfers, stretching develops body awareness and body control, making it easier to learn and perform precise motions— like a golf swing. Swing teachers are always talking about "feeling" the right movement or asking you to perform specific tasks like removing all the tension from your arms. Stretching enhances your ability to do all of that. I've had the opportunity to work with Tiger Woods on several occasions, and what truly separates him from the rest of the pack is

Yoga

Yoga is a five-thousand-year-old practice that uses stretches, postures, focused concentration, and breathing techniques to unify the mind, body, and spirit. It's been clinically proven to reduce stress and help you achieve a more relaxed state by lowering your heart rate and stimulating the release of certain brain chemicals; it even helps your body more efficiently cleanse itself of internal toxins. Yoga requires long periods of concentration and uses movements and poses that build body control, foster muscle balance, improve overall balance and coordination, and increase flexibility and strength, especially in the core muscles, which are essential to golf. For all these reasons, yoga is becoming ever more popular among golfers, including professionals like Gary McCord, Ty Tryon, J. L. Lewis, David Gossett, and Annika Sorenstam. It's certainly a good way to improve your golf game, your fitness, and your state of mind all at once.

his amazing ability to isolate and control individual muscles, a skill he no doubt developed through a lifelong commitment to a steady stretching regimen.

Still, at its primary level stretching is about flexibility, or the ability to move bones, joints, and ligaments—the entire body—through a full range of motion. While that's a good general definition, experts generally break the term down into three categories. *Dynamic flexibility* describes the body's ability to move through a full range of motion by flexing various muscles, such as rotating your arm through a full circle alongside your body. *Active flexibility* requires one to hold a stretch strictly through muscle tension, like lifting your leg and holding it out straight in front of you without resting it on anything. *Passive flexibility* refers to the practice of first achieving and then holding a stretched position—for example, touching your toes or reaching your arms straight up over your head. These are the most basic stretches and the ones people most often associate with stretching and flexibility.

For golfers, the two most important are dynamic and passive (or *static*) flexibility. You need to achieve a full shoulder turn and reach a high finish by swinging the club. In other words, you need a full range

---

Strength-Building Stretches: Isometrics

Yes, stretching can make you stronger. When done properly, isometric stretching improves strength and is by far the most effective way to increase overall flexibility—but doing it properly is not easy. In fact, I don't suggest trying it without the supervision of a qualified expert, such as a personal trainer or physical therapist.

The technique works by combining static stretches with periods of contraction against some sort of resistance. For instance, if you wanted to do an isometric stretch of your calf, you would sit with your legs extended straight out in front of you, grab your toes, then pull them toward you, thereby stretching your calf. But instead of releasing your toes at the end of the stretch, you'd hold on and then actually try pushing your foot away from your body by contracting your calf muscle, as if you were trying to point your toes. This process of flexing into the stretch is the main idea behind isometrics and it can be very effective when done properly.

---

of motion (passive) achieved through active movement (dynamic). This is not to say you should just forget about active flexibility. It's actually a great way to build muscle strength and the best means of achieving Tigeresque muscle control. It's just not as much of a prerequisite for making a good swing.

A lack of any of these types of flexibility can occur for many reasons (injury, bone size, or muscle size, for example) but most often occurs as a defense mechanism because your body resists stretching past the point at which you feel pain. So if you don't stretch often, or ever, it won't take long before it starts to hurt, and your body will resist the movement, therefore limiting your range of motion.

To increase your range of motion, you need more stretching—but *carefully planned* stretching that considers not just when and which muscles to stretch but what type of stretch to do. We'll look at three main types of stretching in this book, *dynamic, active,* and *passive.* As I'm sure you've guessed, each type of stretch corresponds to the types of flexibility described earlier.

As most people know, it's a good idea to stretch before any type of physical activity, whether that's lifting weights, running, or playing golf.

Tom Pernice Jr. on Working Out

Q: What made you decide to start working out?

TP: I just thought it was a way to improve my play and to prolong my playing career. It seemed obvious that increased golf strength and increased overall strength would be an asset.

Q: How did you get started with Boris?

TP: Vijay and I are pretty close, and Vijay knew Boris. So when Boris came over here with Gabe Hjertstedt and started working out, Vijay and I thought it was something that would help, so we both started at the same time.

Q: What kind of impact has it had on you?

TP: I've increased my strength and flexibility dramatically, and I've improved my overall health as well. On the golf course, if you're stronger and more flexible you can swing the club faster and hit the ball farther. It also means that you can hold up better over the course of the season, so you'll be able to play as well in September as you could in May.

Q: Was stamina part of the equation?

TP: Yes, it allows you to play better over a longer period of time and prolongs your career.

Q: What about the mental aspect of the game?

TP: I believe that better conditioning helps you maintain sharper mental focus on the course and allows you to play better. There's no way to prove that, but I, and I think most of the guys on the Tour agree, really feel that way.

Q: How hard is it to stick with the program?

TP: In the beginning it was a sacrifice of time and effort, but Boris was a huge motivator and eventually it became part of my daily routine. It is now a part of my day, and I can't imagine not doing it.

Q: What's the overall effect of the fitness boom on the PGA Tour?

TP: It's become a major part of the game, and it's going to continue to be one. All these athletes coming into the game now are bigger and better and stronger, and they keep themselves in great shape. That's why the ball is flying so much farther out here. It's not the equipment; it's these better athletes who are stronger and swing the club faster, and it's only going to keep going that way.

At forty-three years old, Tom Pernice Jr., a two-time All-American at UCLA, remains a steady fixture on the PGA Tour, racking up his two Tour wins after the age of forty.

Tom Pernice Jr.
(Photo courtesy of The Acushnet Company)

What's less clear to the average person is how to stretch, including when, in what order, and for how long.

The first step is to warm up. Stretching is not warming up. Stretching is part of a good warm-up routine, but it's not all of it. Warming up is about more than loosening muscles; it actually improves performance. Failing to do it increases your risk of injury.

Start by doing some light physical activity—a slow jog, a brisk walk, a few sets of leisurely jumping jacks, a peppy hike out to the driving range. The idea is to achieve two to five minutes of low-level activity to get the heart pumping, the blood flowing, and the muscles warm. Once the muscles are a little loose, you will get a better stretch and reduce your risk of injury.

The next step is to perform a round of static stretches. Keep in mind a few basic principles: Whenever possible, perform stretches that work one muscle at a time and that isolate muscles. In other words, instead of bending to stretch both hamstrings at once, do each one individually. (Details on how to perform specific stretches appear at the end of the chapter.)

Pilates

During World War I, Joseph Pilates had the unenviable task of attempting to rehabilitate injured soldiers who'd spent months wasting away in hospital beds. Many of them had become tremendously weak and had lingering wounds that prevented them from even standing. So Pilates developed a system of exercises that could be done right in a bed and eventually invented a bed-like apparatus that made the workouts even easier and more effective. Today, the system Pilates created is named after him and is one of the most popular exercise methods around.

Drawing from yoga, martial arts, and gymnastics, Pilates concentrates on the "core" muscles of your torso, especially those deep transverse and stabilizing fibers of the pelvis, abdomen, and back. A strong, balanced core lets the rest of your joints and muscles function properly; this is why everyone from ballet dancers to professional athletes as diverse as Jason Kidd and Annika Sorenstam have been drawn to it. Done properly, it can increase your flexibility, strength, balance, coordination, and concentration while improving your overall health and lowering your golf score. What's more, it's a low-impact workout that revolves around stretching and flexibility, which means anyone can do it.

As part of a larger fitness routine or on its own, Pilates has a lot of potential for golfers.

Try to relax as much as possible while stretching and focus on taking deep breaths, exhaling as you initiate the stretch. There's a lot of conflicting research on this, but generally you should try to hold each stretch for ten to twenty seconds and do them in sets of two or three repetitions. Also, you want to start from the center, or core, of your body and work your way from larger to smaller muscle groups. Do the back first, then the torso, neck, upper legs, upper arms, calves, shins, forearms and wrists. If you don't have time to stretch every muscle group, at least carefully stretch the ones you'll be using the most.

Whatever you do, don't force your body into positions it does not want to assume and don't bounce or swing yourself into and out of stretches, a practice known as *ballistic stretching*, which can cause serious injuries. What you should do, though, is some dynamic stretching after the static stretching. These include slow, controlled movements

Breathing During Stretching

Breathing helps the body relax and increases blood flow, which helps the body more efficiently remove unwanted metabolic by-products like lactic acid. Proper breathing should involve long, slow breaths that you draw by expanding your abdomen, not your chest. Likewise, you should inhale and exhale through your nose, but control the air flow with the back of your throat instead of your nostrils, so that you make a sort of deep humming sound rather than a loud sniffing noise. Inhale before beginning the stretch, then exhale as you move fully into the depth of it. Inhale again while holding and then exhale again as you return to the starting position.

that continue to loosen up joints and muscles, such as arm circles, leg circles, and torso twists. Remember to go slow so that what you get is a gentle stretch rather than a pull or strain.

If you're doing a pre-golf warm-up, your next move should be to pull out a club and start doing some light swings, progressing slowly to full practice swings. If it's a pre-workout warm-up, you would now consider yourself ready to dive into the meat of your training. The whole thing shouldn't take more than ten minutes.

At the end of any strenuous activity, you'll want to do a cool-down, which can reduce the muscle soreness that often follows a hard workout. Start the cool-down by gradually slowing down whatever activity you're performing—for example, if you're running, slow down to a fast walk for a few minutes. When you come to a complete stop, do some dynamic stretching while your heart returns to its normal rhythm, then move on to some static stretches.

Specific Stretches and How to Do Them

As it is with many things in golf, when in comes to working out, technique is vitally important. Follow the photos and descriptions closely to ensure that you're performing the movements properly. Doing them wrong can not only make them less effective but actually lead to injuries. Remember, the key is to stretch, not strain.

Lower Back

4.1

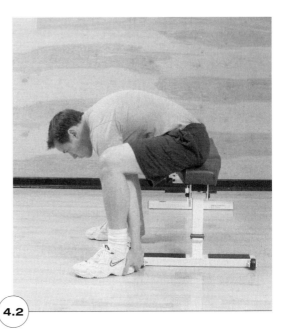

4.2

Sit on a workout bench or firm chair with your knees apart and bent at a 90-degree angle. Lean forward from the waist, not the hips, trying to get your stomach between your legs and to touch the floor between your feet or grab your heels (4.1). For a deeper stretch, once your hands are touching the floor, push the middle of your back toward the ceiling (4.2).

Middle Back

4.3

4.4

Sit on a workout bench or on the floor, back straight, knees bent. Pull your left leg up toward your lap and grab the outside of your left foot with your right hand (4.3). Try to straighten your leg (you won't be fully able to) while holding on (4.4). You will feel the stretch between your shoulder blades. Repeat with the other arm-leg combination.

Side Back

4.5

4.6

Stand straight with your right foot crossed in front of the left. Lift your arms straight up and clasp hands (4.5). Keeping your hips still, lean your body to the right (4.6). You'll feel the stretch down your left side. Reverse your feet and lean in the other direction to stretch the right side.

Neck

4.7

4.8

Sit on a workout bench or firm chair, back straight. Grip the chair under your thigh with your left hand to hold your body upright as you tilt your head to the right (4.7 and 4.8). To get a better stretch put your right hand on top of your head and let the weight rest on it. Don't pull. Repeat on the other side.

Abdominals

4.9

4.10

Lie on your stomach and raise your shoulders off the floor, supporting your upper body with your elbows (4.9). Then push your chest forward and up (4.10).

Hips

4.11

4.12

Hold a workout bench or chair for balance, then lower yourself so that your right knee sits on the floor and your left leg is bent in front of you at a 90-degree angle (4.11). Lean your lower body forward, making sure to keep your upper body perpendicular to the floor (4.12), and feel the stretch down the front of your hip. Repeat on the other side.

Glutes

4.13

4.14

Sit on a workout bench or chair with your back straight, right foot on the floor, and left foot crossed over your right knee (4.13). Both knees should be bent 90 degrees. With your left hand push your left knee down and lean your upper body forward until you feel the stretch in your glutes (4.14). Repeat on the other side.

Front Thigh

4.15

4.16

Hold a workout bench or chair for balance, then lower yourself so that your right knee sits on the floor and your left leg is bent in front of you at a 90-degree angle (4.15). Grab your right ankle and raise it gently toward your back (4.16). Repeat on other side.

Back Thigh

4.17

4.18

Lie on your back holding either end of a rope or towel in each hand. Run the rope or towel under one of your feet (4.17), then straighten your leg and gently pull it toward your head, keeping the opposite leg flat on the floor (4.18). Repeat with the other foot.

Inner Thigh

4.19

4.20

Sit on the floor with your soles together in front of you, your knees bent and pushed out to the sides (4.19). Put your elbows on your knees and slowly lean forward while pushing down with your elbows (4.20).

Calf

4.21   4.22

Stand with your toes on either a step or a box so that the rest of your foot is suspended (4.21). Slowly allow your heels to drop toward the floor as far as possible (4.22).

Chest

4.23

Stand with your right arm straight out to the side, then bend your elbow 90 degrees. Press your hand, forearm, and elbow against a post or door opening, then push your right shoulder and the right side of your chest forward (4.23). Repeat on the other side.

Front Shoulder

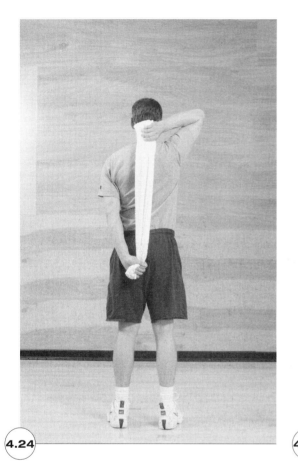

4.24

4.25

Extend your right arm overhead holding a rope or towel. Let your hand drop behind your head, keeping your elbow pointing toward the ceiling. Reach behind your back and grasp the rope or towel with the opposite hand (4.24) and gently pull up (4.25). Repeat on the other side.

Back Shoulder

4.26

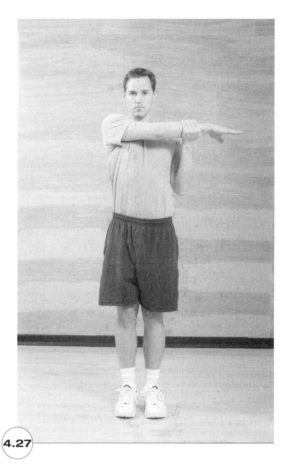

4.27

Standing or seated, extend your right arm straight in front of you. Grab your right elbow with your left hand (4.26) and pull your right arm across your chest (4.27). Repeat on the other side.

Back Arm

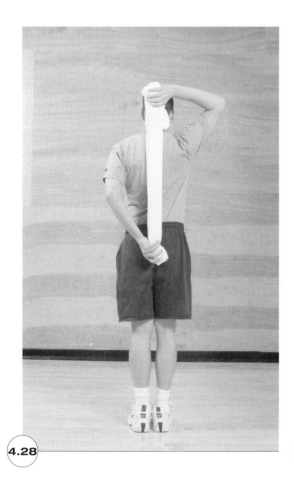

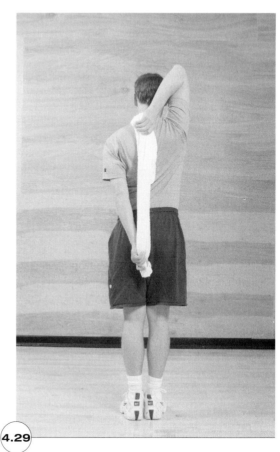

Extend your right arm overhead holding a rope or towel. Let your hand drop behind your head, keeping your elbow pointing toward the ceiling. Reach behind your back and grasp the rope or towel with the opposite hand (4.28) and gently pull down (4.29). Repeat on the other side.

Front Arm

4.30

Stand with your right side to a wall. Keeping your right arm straight, place your palm on the wall behind you at shoulder height (4.30). Turn your body away from the wall. For a better stretch, make a fist, rotate your arm so your thumb points at the floor, then press your knuckles against the wall instead of your palm. Repeat on the other side.

Forearm

4.31

4.32

Kneel and put your hands on the floor in front of you, palms up, fingers toward your body (4.31). Keeping your hands flat on the floor, lift your shoulders and back toward the ceiling. Flip your hands over, palms down, fingers rotated as far as possible to the inside, and again lift with your shoulders and back while keeping hands flat (4.32).

Massage

You already know a massage feels good, but you may not realize that it can actually improve performance and assist healing. A good, deep muscle massage increases blood flow to specific muscles, which makes them looser, relieves built-up tension, eases muscle cramps, and aids in the removal of metabolic waste such as lactic acid. A build-up of lactic acid is part of what makes you sore after a workout, so a massage can help ease that soreness. Loosening and warming the muscles also allows you to get a better stretch and better workout through a more complete range of motion, and a massage before a round of golf would obviously make it easier to execute a big, full swing. If you can't always find the time for a full massage, you can try a little self-massage on the muscles you're about to use immediately before stretching or working out.

Remember, stretching before a workout or round of golf is essential, but it doesn't have to mean your stretching is done for the day. Feel free to continue stretching during either activity, especially if something feels tight or if you have to wait a long time between shots or sets. It's hard to stretch too much, but easy to stretch too little.

Some golfers think that they don't have to stretch at all, because they're "naturally flexible" or because they have a homegrown swing that doesn't look like something you'd see on TV and it doesn't require quite as much twisting and bending. While that may be true, there are still plenty of reasons to stretch. It will not only increase your flexibility, making it easier to swing while improving your control and distance, but it will help you to maintain whatever flexibility you already have, thereby allowing you to play better for a longer period of time.

Furthermore, stretching might be the best way to avoid injury. Golf is unique in that there's no opportunity to start slowly and work your way into the game, like you could if your were running or playing basketball. The first hole often requires you to hit with a driver, the club that calls for the biggest, most taxing swing you can make. In essence, you need to go from 0 to 100 mph right out of the gate. Without some proper warm-up, including stretching, that's difficult and possibly damaging for anyone.

So, no matter who you are and how you swing, don't forget to stretch.

Cardiovascular Fitness

Golf and cardiovascular fitness might seem unrelated, but they are connected. Do you ever find that you start pulling your shots late in the round? When you're tired, you slouch (there's that posture thing again), which causes you to stand with more weight on your heels. And when you've got your weight on your heels, you tend to pull the ball.

What about shot selection? Do you find yourself trying to pull off tough shots late in the round when you know you're better off playing it safe? Fatigue affects decision making. And if you're not getting the same leg drive that you were early in the round, you're not going to get the same distance.

The golf swing requires the controlled coordination of almost all the muscles in your body and a great deal of mental focus. And when you get tired, even so slightly that you don't notice it, it becomes harder and harder to execute. Although it might not require any sustained burst of physical exertion, golf can wear you down.

Just count the swings. If you shoot 80, you probably have about 30 putts per round, which means you take 50 swings. Add a practice swing before each, and that brings you to about 100 swings. Do you take more than one practice swing? Do you go to the driving range before you play? Do you shoot higher than 80? Add all those swings in as well and you're talking about somewhere between 150 and 300 swings.

Then there's the walking. Even those golfers who drive a golf cart right up to their ball so they don't have to walk more than two feet still have to mount eighteen tees and amble out onto eighteen greens. Then you have the cart-path-only days that force cart riders to walk almost as much as someone carrying a bag. For those who do walk, the average golf course is between five and six miles long—a pretty healthy sojourn, especially when you are carrying or pulling a thirty-pound bag of clubs.

And don't forget to consider time. Golf takes place over a four- or five-hour span and requires near-constant mental focus. As anyone who's taken the SAT can attest, the simple act of concentrating for five hours can wear you out mentally as well as physically.

Add all those factors together and you can see the need for cardio-vascular conditioning. A good cardiovascular program will not only improve your heart and lung function, it will increase your muscle stamina and add other physical benefits. It lowers your blood pressure and your resting heart rate, which means your heart does not have to work as hard. It bolsters your immune system, helping you stave off illness and recover faster when you do get sick. Likewise, it helps prevent injuries and the effects of stress and speeds the recovery from them as well. Moreover, it increases mental stamina and allows you to work harder for longer periods of time.

How hard you have to work to achieve those benefits and where you begin depends on what kind of shape you're in now. A Surgeon General's report says thirty minutes of accumulated activity—walking, taking the stairs, gardening, sex—most every day can deliver the kind of health benefits associated with an "active" lifestyle. Certainly, this kind of daily activity makes a great starting point for anyone who's totally out of shape. You can even work golf into the mix.

Maybe there's no way you can walk eighteen, especially on a hot, humid day, but you can always walk a little. After you hit your tee shot, let your playing partner take the cart out to the ball while you walk. You don't have to pull or carry a bag, but you still get the benefit of the exercise. Or maybe follow all your wedge shots into the green. Hit it on, then walk up. Or you and a cart partner can take turns, alternately walking and riding on each hole. This way, you start to build up your strength and stamina while you're playing. Remember, golf started out as a walking sport, and just because carts are available doesn't mean you should pass up the chance to get a little exercise.

You may even find you like it better. I know many golfers who feel they play better and enjoy the round more when they walk. They're somehow more involved and closer to the course when they walk. It gives them more time to think about what they want to do and to appreciate being outside on a big, beautiful piece of land.

So gradually increasing your activity will get you started, but once you're past that initial phase of physical fitness you're going to have to step it up a notch in order to improve your fitness and therefore your game. For that, you'll need twenty to forty minutes of moderate exercise at least three times a week. To achieve weight loss or get to the next level of fitness, the American College of Sports Medicine recommends thirty to forty-five minutes of moderate to hard exercise four times per week or more.

But here's the catch: not all cardiovascular exercise is the same. In general it's broken down into two categories, *aerobic* and *anaerobic*. *Aerobic* workouts are long-duration, low-intensity grinds that promote weight loss and improve the intake of oxygen and the blood's capacity to carry it throughout the body, making the entire system more efficient and capable of doing more work with less effort (for example, jogging). *Anaerobic* workouts are short, high-intensity jolts that increase lung capacity, improve muscle endurance, and even build muscle mass (for example, running sprints). Ideally, a good cardiovascular fitness program will employ both. The best way to achieve that is through something called *interval training*, in which you combine each type of workout in separate intervals. For example, we'll pretend you're riding a stationary bicycle. You might just pedal for twenty-five minutes at a steady pace

Definitions

Aerobic workout. Long-term steady exertion at somewhere between 60 and 80 percent of maximum heart rate that increases heart and lung efficiency and burns fat

Anaerobic workout. Short-term, high-intensity activity at approximately 90 percent of maximum heart rate that builds muscle endurance and mass

Cross-training. Using multiple methods of working out in order to keep your interest level up and provide fresh challenges for your body, such as playing basketball one day, swimming the next, and running the next

Interval training. Process of mixing aerobic and anaerobic workouts to make them more efficient and vastly increase your growth and stamina

Maximum heart rate. In theory, the highest number of times your heart can beat per minute as a result of physical exertion

Target heart rate. The number of heartbeats per minute someone attempts to achieve or maintain as part of a workout plan (for example, 130 beats per minute equals 70 percent of maximum for a thirty-five-year-old)

that keeps your pulse at about 70 percent of your maximum heart rate, a classic aerobic workout.

But in order to get more out of your time and build your body in multiple ways, you can break up your steady twenty-five-minute ride with brief bursts, up to a minute or so, of very fast pedaling that brings your pulse up to about 90 percent of your maximum heart rate. When the minute is up, you drop back down to the 60- to 70-percent range and keep going. Ideally, you'd go about four minutes at an aerobic level followed by a one-minute anaerobic burst. This not only provides you the advantage of blending both types of workout but forces you to keep pedaling at an aerobic level even as you're recovering from the anaerobic interval, which is an incredibly effective means of building lung capacity.

Don't let all that stuff about maximum heart rates and percentages overwhelm you. First, most gym equipment has technology built in that helps you track maximum heart rate. Whether it's a stationary bicycle, stairclimber, treadmill, or rowing machine, many of the newer machines have clocks, resistance level indicators, and heart rate monitors built right in. Most even have preprogrammed interval settings that will automatically increase and decrease the resistance to give you a challenging aerobic-anaerobic mix.

If you don't have access to this kind of equipment, there are alternative ways to measure intensity. You can purchase a heart rate monitor, a small, inexpensive piece of equipment that straps around your wrist or your chest and tells you exactly how fast your heart is beating. Or, as you become more familiar with your body's capacity you can use a less scientific but good method of estimation. The rule of thumb states that during a "light" workout you'll probably just break a sweat and feel little strain in your muscles. If you're moving pretty well, working up a sweat and pushing it a bit, but can still read or comfortably hold a conversation, you're most likely at the level of a moderate or aerobic workout. When it becomes difficult to speak and you're really straining, then you've hit the high-intensity anaerobic category.

As far as figuring out maximum heart rate and target heart rates for various workouts, a simple equation will help. Estimate your maximum heart rate by subtracting your age from 220 (see "Heart Math" on the next page). Multiply that number by the heart rate percentage desired (expressed as a decimal) to come up with your target heart rate. The method is not exact, but it is simple and accurate enough to form the basis for building a workout.

Beyond that, what kind of exercise you do is entirely up to you. Options include anything from running, which is outdoors and free, to joining a fancy gym with all the latest equipment. Either serves the purpose as long as you're willing to work at it a little.

It also helps to be smart about your approach. Several tips will help you stick with it and make your workout time more productive.

Choose things that you like to do. If you hate the stairclimber, don't use it in your workout. Also, don't be afraid to switch from one type of exercise to another. Whether it's running one day, swimming the next, and basketball the next, combining different types of exercise, a practice known as *cross-training*, not only makes working out more fun and

Heart Math

To calculate your maximum heart rate and target heart rate, use the following simple formula. Then use a heart rate monitor (many machines have them built in) to adjust your workout so that you're exercising at an appropriate number of beats per minute. For a light workout you'd want 40 to 50 percent of maximum; a moderate or aerobic workout is 60 to 70 percent; and a hard or anaerobic workout is 80 to 90 percent of your maximum heart rate. (Always begin in the "light" category and work your way up.) The equation is as follows:

Maximum heart rate: 220 minus your age

For example, a thirty-five-year-old would subtract 35 from 220.

220 − 35 = 185

Target heart rate: Maximum heart rate times the desired percentage expressed as a decimal (for example, 70 percent = 0.7)

185 × 0.7 = 130

So a thirty-five-year-old looking to work out at 70 percent of his or her capacity would shoot for a heart rate of about 130 beats per minute.

interesting (which increases the chances you'll do it), it has benefits for the body.

Different activities stress your body in different ways, which provides a better overall workout. For instance, running and riding a bicycle both work your legs, but they focus on different muscles in your legs and stress the joints and ligaments in different ways, which strengthens everything and provides a better overall workout. Also, as with most things, your body quickly adapts to challenges. So if you start out riding the bike for twenty minutes, it won't be long before that workout no longer provides the same benefits or challenges it originally did. Confronting your body with a steady stream of new challenges will make your workouts more efficient and get you in better overall shape.

For the same reason, you should continue to adjust the parameters of your workout. When you feel or see on your heart rate monitor that

---

Finding Intervals

Traditional workout equipment or exercises allow you to manufacture your own intervals. You can dictate your own pace while running, riding, rowing, or any other exercise, timing your aerobic periods and mixing in intervals of high-intensity work to maximize your workouts. But many sports naturally create interval workouts, such as basketball, soccer, and tennis. All these sports involve a long period of moderate aerobic activity interspersed with brief bursts of high-output action. Don't forget to consider these sports when designing your own fitness plan. It's one way to take the work out of workout.

---

your twenty-minute bike ride is no longer giving you a worthy aerobic challenge, you should make it tougher. Start by increasing the duration. Go to twenty-five minutes, and then thirty. Once you get comfortable at thirty, increase the intensity, either by increasing the resistance level on the machine or quickening your pace. Even if you can't go at the new level for the entire time, start slowly and work your way up. Go the first ten minutes at a higher level, then back down to the old level for the next twenty. Keep building until you can do the entire workout at the increased intensity level. Then start over.

As you do this, it won't take long to see changes in your body, your golf game, and your life. You'll probably slim down a bit. You'll be able to walk eighteen holes and still feel strong and fresh at the end. Overall, you'll get fewer colds, recover from them faster, and reduce your risk factor for a long list of diseases and life-threatening conditions. Moreover, you'll feel stronger, healthier, and better about yourself, giving you a confidence that will spill over into everything you do.

Programs

The following programs are designed to help increase both aerobic and then eventually anaerobic fitness. Anaerobic fitness does not play a big role in golf so don't worry if you never get there, but it is a part of good overall fitness and a worthy goal to pursue, however slowly and steadily your body can.

Beginner

Start by going for walks. Try to keep the pace crisp and steady so that you feel your heart rate quicken a bit and you build a light sweat. If you have a heart rate monitor, maintain approximately 40 to 50 percent of your maximum heart rate. Try to go for thirty minutes, but if you can't make it that far, work your way up slowly. Keep at it until you can go for thirty to forty-five minutes at a heart rate of about 50 percent. Do this at least three times a week—more, if possible. When you can complete the program comfortably, transition to a moderate program.

Moderate

Three or four times a week perform twenty minutes of aerobic exercise, keeping your heart rate between 60 and 80 percent of maximum. When you can comfortably complete twenty minutes and your heart rate begins to drop toward the lower end of that range, increase the duration until you can do thirty minutes. When you can comfortably do thirty minutes, increase the intensity, even if it's only for part of the time. Keep building until you can go for thirty minutes at the higher level. When you can complete the program comfortably, transition to an advanced program.

Advanced

Begin interval training. Continue your normal aerobic workout level, then mix in short periods of high-output exercise where your heart rate reaches up to 90 percent of maximum. Over a twenty-five-minute workout, try half a minute of high-output exercise for every six minutes of moderate exercise. Gradually increase to one-minute periods of high output. Once this is accomplished, start decreasing the time between intervals: one minute of high for every five minutes of moderate, then one to four, and one to three.

6

Strength Training

Like stretching, strength training offers multiple benefits. If done right, it reduces the risk of injury and post-injury recovery time. Once you've been at it a while, it reduces muscle soreness after any kind of activity, increases muscle control, and improves performance. Moreover, good muscle development adds to better overall health by bolstering the immune system, increasing stamina, and making it easier to do more, a physical benefit that allows you to stay sharper mentally. It counteracts some of the effects of aging by maintaining bone density and muscle mass. And because muscle requires more energy to exist than fat, the more muscle you have the more calories you burn by just existing—a metabolic coup that can help you burn calories and lose weight even while you're sitting around watching TV.

Most important, though, balanced muscle development (as discussed in Chapter 2) allows you to exert equal or greater power with less effort. The importance of such a function for golfers can't be overstated. The enemy of every golf swing is tension. Tension in your hands, your wrists, your arms, even in your back and legs, to say nothing of your mind, can wreak havoc on a golf swing. This is why every golf instruction book or TV show advises that you grip the club lightly (no tension in your hands), waggle the club (loosen any tension in the wrists and arms), and stand with your weight slightly forward and your knees gently flexed, like a shortstop (to relieve any tension in your legs and back).

All that is great advice, but the reality is that out on the course every golfer feels that need for a little more distance. Maybe you're between clubs, or you're trying to impress your playing partners, or you're in the rough or the heavy sand and you end up trying to put a little extra into the swing. A little more oomph, a little more turn, a little more push and pull. And that little more, that effort, equals tension, which usually means you're going to hit the ball with less power and have less control over it.

The beauty of strength is that it lets you generate more clubhead speed and hit the ball harder without introducing tension into your swing. Good muscle development and proper muscle balance allow you to do more with less effort so you can keep your muscles relaxed while they exert more power, which is the key to hitting long, straight shots. In addition, there are circumstances in which pure raw strength is a benefit, such as a buried lie, deep rough, or heavy sand. In such cases you have to either force the club through the impediment or try to play out at an easier angle that won't necessarily get you any closer to the hole. Which option you select and whether your shot will work often comes down to whether you're strong enough to force the club through and still make solid contact. If you're not strong enough, the grass or sand can twist or slow the clubhead so much that the ball goes nowhere, or somewhere even worse.

This is one of the areas in which players like Tiger Woods and Ernie Els have such a clear advantage over guys like Davis Love III or Sergio Garcia. Off a tee or cushy fairway lie, all four of them can hit it a mile—but when they get to the U.S. Open, with its treacherous, deep rough, physically stronger guys like Tiger and Ernie have a better chance of hitting good shots out of the bad stuff. Of course, such shots often come with a fair risk of injury, and the stronger you are the less your chances of getting hurt.

Swing Trainers

Along with golf's fitness boom have come a number of workout contraptions aimed at golfers. There seem to be two basic types: the overhead apparatus with a grip that dangles from a pulley or elastic band of some sort, and the freestanding swing trainer that's either weighted or offers wind resistance. These devices may or may not be effective at training certain muscles involved in the swing, but what they certainly won't do is provide the sort of good overall fitness and muscle balance I advocate both for better health and a better golf game. Using these devices in both directions (swinging lefty and righty) will certainly provide some degree of balance in the active muscles, but it will do nothing for the muscles that are inactive. That kind of training probably won't help all aspects of your life and game as much as a good overall workout program.

I call this "swinging easier with more power," and the road that ends there starts in the weight room. Using the exercises suggested in this chapter, you can develop a program that will make you stronger and more fit, and with a little tweaking you can fine-tune it to suit the particular needs of your body. Remember that working out does carry a risk of injury, so before beginning any form of physical exercise you should undergo a full physical and consult with a certified personal trainer to make sure the exercises you've chosen work well together and that you're performing them properly.

There are a few general things to bear in mind about working out with weights. First, momentum kills. When you're lifting weights, the point is to perform the motion correctly while moving the weights slowly through their complete range. This often means you have to start with less weight than you think you should, and if you go to a gym you'll have to deal with the intimidation of seeing people around you using heavier weights. You'll be tempted to increase your weights so as not to seem weak in comparison. Don't do it.

First, most of those people lifting the heavy weight complete the motion much too rapidly and use momentum to help them do the exercise. Those little swings and bounces may not seem like much, but they rob you of a complete workout because your muscles are not working throughout the entire lift, which creates a false sense of strength and can lead to muscle imbalances.

Second, you actually build muscle by injuring it. It's similar to breaking a bone. When the bone heals, the spot where the break occurred is actually stronger than the rest. When you lift weights you cause dozens of *microtears* to the muscle fiber. After the workout, the body sets about repairing these tears, and as it does, the repaired muscle emerges stronger. Repeated over and over, the tiny injuries cause the muscles to grow noticeably stronger, firmer, and larger.

This is why it's essential to take a day off after a workout: the time allows your body to heal and rebuild itself before the next assault. It's also another reason momentum prevents you from getting the best workout you can. When you bounce or swing the weights, at least part of the muscle in action doesn't have to do its share of the work. Trying to lift too much weight not only forces you to use momentum but makes the muscle in question recruit help from other muscles instead of doing the work itself, and that's a perfect recipe for muscle imbalance.

For instance, imagine you are doing a dumbbell curl. As you start to lower the weight the top of your bicep does most of the work, then the middle part kicks in, and as you come to rest at the bottom the lower part of the muscle takes over. But most people don't do it that way. They stop resisting about six inches from the bottom of the motion, letting the weight freefall and swing past the body. As the momentum starts to swing back forward, they then flex the muscle again and begin to lift. This practice makes it easier to complete the lift, and looks better in front of everyone at the gym, but it requires less work of the entire muscle and especially the lowest third. You'd be better off doing a slower rep with less weight and keeping steady resistance throughout the entire range. Slowing it down also has the benefit of forcing you to control the weight better, which builds that all-important muscle control and reduces the risk of injury.

In addition, lower weights with higher repetitions build strength and tone as opposed to size, and in a sport like golf, bulky muscles that can't get out of their own way are a definite disadvantage. This doesn't mean you should never add weight. When completing your sets, the last few reps should be difficult. If they are not, you should consider adding weight. You may be able to do fewer reps after the initial increase, say 10 instead of 12 or 15, but that's OK. Slowly build your way back up, and when it becomes easy again, increase the weight some more.

That same philosophy applies to medicine ball training. Although this training is often overlooked here in the United States, a good medicine ball routine can be one of the best ways to get a sport-specific workout. Because the balls bounce and you can throw and catch them, they allow you to train in ways and develop attributes not allowed by standard weight training. When done right, a medicine ball session will develop strength, flexibility, coordination, endurance, balance, explosive muscle response, rhythm, focus, and sport-specific muscle memory. In addition, medicine balls develop your core, the deep structural muscles of your abdomen and torso that stabilize your body and add power to the most basic of movements.

Leg Exercises

Squat

Works the entire lower body, especially the front and back of the upper thigh and the buttocks.

6.1

6.2

Instruction: Grasp a bar outside shoulder width and rest it across the back of your shoulders (6.1). Stand and step clear of the rack. Pick a spot directly in front of you and a little bit higher than eye level and focus on it throughout the set. Keeping your back absolutely straight, take a deep breath and squat down as far as you can but not past the point where your thighs are almost parallel with the floor (6.2). Make sure your knees and toes point in the same direction throughout. Exhale and push back up to the starting position.

@home: Squats are also effective if done in high numbers without any weight, or even while holding a medicine ball.

Leg Extension

Works the front of the thigh.

6.3

6.4

Instruction: Adjust machine so that leg pads are at ankle height and the back of the thigh is all the way on the seat (6.3). Hold onto the sides of the seat and slowly extend your legs (6.4). Hold for a moment at the top, then slowly lower.

Leg Curl
Works the back of the upper thigh.

6.5   6.6

Instruction: Sit on the machine so that your knees hang just off the edge of the pad and adjust leg pads so that they press just above the heels (6.5). Push the weight down slowly, hold, then let it rise just as slowly (6.6). (If your gym has a lying-down machine, be sure your hips stay down during the lift.)

Modified Deadlift
Works the back of the legs and buttocks.

6.7

6.8

Instruction: Stand on the floor with the bar in front of you. Keeping your back straight, your eyes forward, and your legs slightly bent, lean forward at the hips, grasp the bar, and return to a standing position in a slow, controlled movement (6.7). Lower the bar through the same range of motion until you feel a stretch in the back of your legs (6.8). When you no longer feel a stretch, try grasping the bar while standing on a box with your toes touching the edge (as if it were a diving board) to increase the range of motion.

Lunge

Works the front of the thigh and the buttocks.

6.9

6.10

Instruction: Stand with a dumbbell in each hand (6.9). Keeping your back straight and your eyes focused on a spot in front of you, take a long stride forward with your right leg and lunge so that your left knee touches the ground and your right knee forms a right angle (6.10). Make sure your body remains upright and your toe and knee point in the same direction throughout. Push off with the right leg to return to the start. Repeat on the opposite side.

@home: Do lunges without weights or while holding a medicine ball in front of you. Swing the ball to the opposite side of the foot going forward on each step.

Standing Calf Press
Works the entire calf.

Instruction: Stand on a step or box with only your toes so that the rest of your foot is suspended. Hold the weight across your shoulders or at your sides. Keeping your back straight and your stomach muscles contracted, push up on your toes as high as you can (6.11), hold for a moment, then slowly lower yourself as far as you can go (6.12).

Sitting Calf Press
Works the lower calf muscle.

6.13

6.14

Instruction: Sit on a bench with a weight across your legs and your feet elevated on a step or block. Keeping your back straight, stomach contracted, and knees directly above your feet, push up on your toes as high as you can (6.13), hold for a moment, then slowly lower your heels as far as you can (6.14).

Back Exercises

Lat Pull (Wide Grip)
Works the entire back and the lower neck.

6.15

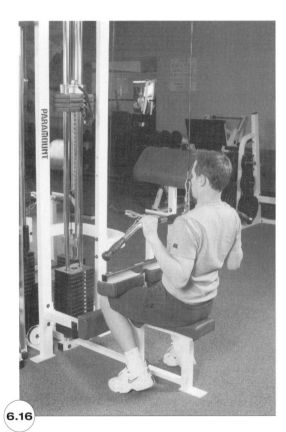

6.16

Instruction: Grasp the bar wider than shoulder width, keeping your chest high and your shoulders down (6.15). Pull the bar down to your chest slowly (6.16), pause, then let it rise again slowly. Keep your body still throughout the movement.

@home: Pull-ups (palms-forward grip) are a great substitute. If you can't do many at first, put one foot on a bench or chair to reduce the resistance.

Lat Pull (Narrow Grip)

Works the lower back and the front of the arms.

6.17

6.18

Instruction: Use a narrow V-shaped bar or grasp a regular bar with hands almost touching (6.17). Keeping your chest high and your shoulders down, pull the bar down to your chest slowly (6.18), pause, then let it rise again slowly. Keep your body still throughout the movement.

Seated Row

Works the entire back.

Instruction: Use a narrow V-shaped handle or a narrow grip on a standard bar. Keep knees slightly bent, back straight, stomach tight. Lean forward and grasp the bar (6.19), then work in three distinct moves: sit back to upright, squeeze your shoulder blades together, then pull your hands to your stomach (6.20). Hold briefly, then reverse.

Dumbbell Row
Works the entire back.

Instruction: Stand on your right foot with your left knee and left hand leaning on a workout bench. Grasp a dumbbell with your right hand (6.21), squeeze your shoulder blades together, then pull the dumbbell up to the side of your chest so your elbow points at the ceiling (6.22).

Back Extension
Works the lower back.

6.23

6.24

Instruction: Lie on your stomach with your hands at your sides (6.23). Slowly raise your shoulders and chest off the ground, but don't lift too far, just enough so that you can feel the muscles in your lower back contract (6.24). (Note: If you have lower back pain, ask a personal trainer, physical therapist, or qualified fitness professional about an alternative to this exercise.)

Chest Exercises

Incline Dumbbell Press
Works the entire chest, the shoulders, and the back of the arms.

6.25

6.26

Instruction: Sit on the bench with one dumbbell next to each side of the chest (6.25). Slowly push the dumbbells straight up (6.26) and then lower them back down. Make sure to keep your lower back against the bench.

Bench Press

Works the entire chest, the shoulders, and the back of the arms.

Instruction: Lie on a bench. Grasp the bar wider than shoulder width. Slowly lower it until it touches your chest (6.27), then push it back up (6.28). Keep your lower back against the bench; putting your feet up on the bench will help.

Push-Up
Works the entire chest, the shoulders, and the back of the arms.

6.29

6.30

Instruction: Lie on the floor with palms down next to your shoulders (6.29). Tighten your back and abdomen muscles, then push yourself up until your arms are straight (6.30). The last thing to leave the floor should be your chest, and it should be the only thing to touch when you come down between reps.

Shoulder Exercises

Sitting Dumbbell Press
Works the front and outside of the shoulders.

6.31   **6.32**

Instruction: Sit up as straight as possible (with back support or without) holding dumbbells next to your shoulders with palms forward (6.31). Push the weights straight up (6.32), then lower them until they touch the outside of the shoulders.

Lateral Raise
Works the outside of the shoulders and neck.

6.33

6.34

Instruction: Stand or sit with a straight back holding one dumbbell in each hand, arms slightly bent (6.33). Slowly raise the dumbbells out to the side until your arms are parallel to the floor (6.34). At the top of the movement your shoulders should be rotated so that your palm is down and your pinky is slightly higher than your forefinger, as if you were pouring milk.

Dumbbell Shoulder Raise

Works the back of the shoulders.

6.35

6.36

Instruction: Sit on the edge of a chair or workout bench with your feet together directly in front of you. Place dumbbells behind your feet, then bend over and grasp them so that you have a slight bend in your elbow (6.35). Holding your body steady, raise the dumbbells up and slightly forward until they are parallel to the floor or just slightly higher (6.36).

Arm Exercises

Lying Triceps Press
Works the back of the upper arm.

6.37

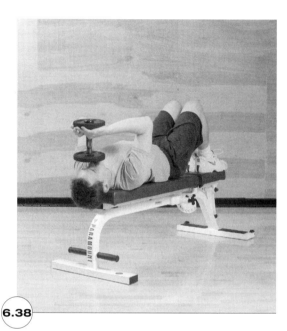

6.38

Instruction: Lie on a bench so your head hangs off the end. Hold a dumbbell lengthwise in both hands directly above your chest, arms straight (6.37). Keeping your elbows stationary and your wrists straight, lower the dumbbell by bending your elbows until it touches your forehead or nose (6.38), then push it back up.

@home: Try doing push-ups with your hands about two inches apart and angled toward each other at about 45 degrees.

Cable Push-Down

Works the back of the upper arm.

Instruction: Grasp a V-shaped cable bar with elbows at your sides (6.39). Keeping your elbows stationary and your wrists straight, push the bar down until your arms are straight (6.40), then slowly let it rise back up.

Dip

Works the back of the upper arm.

Instruction: Position two benches or chairs across from each other. Sit on one and put your feet on the other. Wrap your hands around the bench on either side of your hips (6.41). Keeping your back straight, abdomen tight, and chin up, lower yourself until your elbows form a right angle (6.42). Push back up.

Sitting Dumbbell Curl

Works the front of the upper arm.

Instruction: Sit with your back straight and dumbbells in each hand, arms hanging at your sides (6.43). Bending at the elbow, slowly raise each hand up to your shoulders, making sure to keep your elbows stationary (6.44). Lower the weight slowly and don't swing it at the bottom of the motion.

Standing Bar Curl

Works the front of the upper arm.

6.45

6.46

Instruction: Standing, grasp a bar just outside hip width, palms up (6.45). Slowly curl the bar up to your chest, keeping your back straight and your elbows stationary (6.46).

@home: Try pull-ups with your palms facing toward you.

Forearm Curl
Works the front and back of the lower arm.

Instruction: Sit on a bench and place your forearms on it so that your hands dangle off the end, grasping a bar with palms up. Slowly lower your wrists as far as they will go (6.47) and then curl them back up as high as they will go (6.48). To work the other side of the arm, reverse your grip so your palms face down.

Abdominal Exercises

Crunch
Works the upper abdominals.

Instruction: Lie on your back with your feet up on a chair or workout bench, knees at a 90-degree angle and hands clasped behind your head. Keeping your elbows pointed out to the side and being careful not to pull with your arms, lift your shoulders and chest toward your knees as far as you can go, then slowly lower yourself back to the start.

Hip Tilt
Works the lower abdominals.

Instruction: Lie on your back on a workout bench, holding onto either side with your hands above your head. Lift your legs so that they point straight up in the air. Roll your hips and lower back off the bench as if you were trying to put your feet on the ceiling. Slowly lower your hips back to the starting position and repeat.

@home: At home you can do this one by lying on the floor and holding onto the underside of a couch or heavy chair.

Medicine Ball Exercises
All the medicine ball exercises in this chapter can be done alone or with a partner. Alone, start about two to three feet away from the wall for the standing throws and one to two feet for the sitting throws. In the beginning, consider doing double or almost double the amount from your weak side until you feel as strong and in control from either side. Otherwise, start with the lightest ball you can find (five pounds or less), and when you can do twenty good throws from both sides, take one step farther away from the wall. Keep moving back until you can do twenty per side from seven or eight feet away, then move to a heavier ball and start the process over. These exercises will build strength, give you a good stretch, and provide cardiovascular exertion. Plus, they require balance, rhythm, timing, and focus, so they're perfect for golf.

Swing Throw
Works all the golf muscles.

6.49

6.50

6.51

Instruction: Stand with your side to a wall and assume a golf stance: feet shoulder-width apart, knees bent, leaning slightly forward at the hips, hands on either side of the medicine ball, which hangs in front of you (6.49). Take the ball back as if you were making a backswing, turning your shoulders and hips until your arms are just past parallel to the floor (6.50). Start forward by opening the hip closest to the wall and then swinging through with your upper body. As you come forward, release the ball so that it bounces off the wall and comes back to you (6.51). Catch it and take it back through the original swing path. Maintain the fundamentals of a solid golf swing throughout the movement.

Front Throw

Works the hips and sides of the torso.

6.52 6.53 6.54

Instruction: Stand facing a wall and assume a golf stance, holding the ball in both hands in front of you (6.52). Rotate away from the wall to one side (6.53), then twist back toward the wall, releasing the ball and catching it (6.54).

Basketball Throw

Works the chest, shoulders, and arms.

Instruction: Stand facing a wall, holding the ball in both hands at chest height (6.55). Push straight out with both hands until arms are fully extended, then release to throw (6.56). Catch the ball off the wall.

Elevated Swing Twist

Works the muscles of the hips, sides, and abdomen.

6.57   6.58   6.59

Instruction: Assume the golf stance with your side to a wall, but hold the ball at shoulder height with your arms extended (6.57). Slowly rotate 90 degrees away from the wall, twisting both your hips and shoulders (6.58). As you come forward and rotate to face the wall, release the ball so that it bounces off the wall and comes back to you (6.59).

Back Throw

Works the sides of the torso, shoulders, arms, and back.

6.60

6.61

Instruction: Sit with your back to a wall holding the ball to one side (6.60). Turn your upper body in the opposite direction toward the wall (6.61), releasing the ball behind you.

Lifting Twist Throw

Works the hips, shoulders, torso, and back.

6.62

6.63

Instruction: Sit with your side to a wall, legs almost straight, bent forward at the hips, holding the ball to your side opposite the wall (6.62). Rotate toward the wall, lifting and twisting to the release point (6.63). Catch and repeat.

Programs

In this chapter, I've put together a few sample programs that you might want to use as is or as a guideline for customizing your own routine. They are very general routines designed to help a wide range of people improve overall condition, muscle balance, and, with any luck, golf scores. Once you've identified a routine that seems right for you, consult Chapters 4, 5, and 6 for specific instructions on how to perform the exercises. As noted elsewhere in this book, you may want to tweak your specific workouts to fit the needs of your body, your game, or your available time and equipment. I suggest working with a personal trainer for this type of customization to make sure you're performing all the exercises properly. Likewise, you should always consult a physician for a medical thumbs-up before starting any exercise routine.

Beyond that, start slowly. Some of these programs are designed for people just starting out, but they can be tough on your body if you've been inactive for some time. Try doing fewer sets with less weight than you think appropriate for the first few sessions. At the same time, don't let sore muscles convince you to quit. They're part of the game, and once you get into your routine, that day-after soreness should go away.

At Home (Three or Four Times Per Week)

This program is for those who don't have access to a gym or much money to spend on equipment. (Note: Medicine balls come in weights ranging from a half pound to fifteen pounds and can be purchased in most sporting goods stores for as little as fifteen dollars. Pick one that feels comfortably light and work your way up to a heavier one slowly.)

Warm-Up
A typical warm-up includes five to seven minutes of light cardiovascular exercise and light stretching of all muscles, but especially the ones you'll be working that day. See Chapter 4 for details about warming up. Also, all cardio sessions should include a two- to three-minute cool-down period. All exercises should be done with a knowledgeable spotter.

Cardio
Walk, jog, or ride a bicycle 15 to 30 minutes as described in the cardio programs detailed in Chapter 5.

Strength Training
Shoot for 3 sets of 12 to 20 reps.
- Medicine ball squat
- Medicine ball lunge
- Push-up
- Crunch
- Hip tilt
- All the medicine ball throws

Stretching
Do all the stretches detailed at the end of Chapter 4.

One-Day Wonder

This program is for those who don't have time to work out more than one day a week.

Warm-Up

Cardio
Walk, jog, or ride a bicycle 15 to 30 minutes as described in the cardio programs detailed in Chapter 5.

Strength Training
Shoot for 3 sets of 12 to 20 reps.
- Bench press
- Lat pull (wide grip)
- Lateral raise
- Dip
- Standing bar curl
- Back extension
- Crunch
- Squat
- Leg curl
- Standing calf press
- Forearm curl
- Swing throw
- Front throw

Stretching
Do all the stretches detailed at the end of Chapter 4.

Two-Day Tornado
For those who can work out only twice a week.

First Day

Warm-Up

Cardio
Walk, jog, or ride a bicycle 15 to 30 minutes as described in the cardio programs detailed in Chapter 5.

Strength Training
Shoot for 3 sets of 10 to 15 reps.

- Squat
- Leg extension
- Leg curl
- Modified deadlift
- Standing calf press
- Swing throw
- Front throw
- Crunch

Stretching
- Low back
- Hips
- Glutes
- Front thighs
- Back thighs
- Inner thighs
- Calves
- Abs

Second Day

Warm-Up

Cardio
Walk, jog, or ride a bicycle 15 to 30 minutes as described in the cardio programs detailed in Chapter 5.

Strength Training
Shoot for 3 sets of 10 to 15 reps.
- Bench press
- Incline dumbbell press
- Lat pull (wide grip)
- Seated row
- Back extension
- Lateral raise
- Lying triceps press
- Sitting dumbbell curl

- Lifting twist throw
- Back throw

Stretching
- Low back
- Glutes
- Middle back
- Side back
- Chest
- Neck
- Front shoulder
- Back shoulder
- Back arm
- Front arm
- Forearms

Beginners (Three Times Per Week)

This program is for those who are starting on a workout program for the first time or who have worked out in the past but are currently out of shape. I call this the *80-rep workout*. The idea is to take less weight than you think you need and try to do 80 reps in 1 set. You shouldn't be able to do it. Just keep going until you can't anymore. In fact, if you can do 60 in the first set, you should use more weight. If you get 80 in 2 sets, increase the weight. Ideally, if you have the right weight, it will take you 3 sets to get to 80 reps. If it takes more sets, use less weight. Once you settle on an appropriate weight, stick with it until you can do all 80 in one shot, and then increase the weight. Keep at it for the first three to six weeks, depending on when you feel you're ready to advance to the standard three-day-per-week workout. This will make you sore for the first week or two. Don't give up!

Warm-Up

Cardio
Walk, jog, or ride a bicycle 15 to 30 minutes as described in the cardio programs detailed in Chapter 5.

Strength Training
Work toward 1 set of 80 reps.

- Bench press
- Seated row
- Lateral raise
- Cable push-down
- Sitting dumbbell curl
- Leg extension
- Leg curl
- Crunch (3 sets of 15 to 20)

Stretching
Do all the stretches detailed at the end of Chapter 4.

Standard (Three Times Per Week)

This program is for those who are already in reasonably good shape.

First Day

Warm-Up

Cardio
If you have advanced enough in your cardio training, do one day of high-intensity interval work. Otherwise, walk, jog, or ride a bicycle 15 to 30 minutes as described in the cardio programs detailed in Chapter 5.

Strength Training
Shoot for 3 sets of 10 to 15 reps.

- Bench press
- Incline dumbbell press
- Push-up
- Sitting dumbbell press
- Lateral raise
- Lying triceps press
- Cable push-down

- Dip
- Swing throw
- Front throw

Stretching
- Low back
- Glutes
- Back thighs
- Chest
- Front shoulder
- Back shoulder
- Back arm

Second Day

Warm-Up

Cardio
Walk, jog, or ride a bicycle 15 to 30 minutes as described in the cardio programs detailed in Chapter 5.

Strength Training
Shoot for 3 sets of 10 to 15 reps.
- Lat pull (wide grip)
- Lat pull (narrow grip)
- Seated row
- Dumbbell row
- Dumbbell shoulder raise
- Back extension
- Sitting dumbbell curl
- Standing bar curl
- Forearm curl
- Swing throw
- Front throw

Stretching
- Low back
- Glutes

- Back thighs
- Middle back
- Side back
- Back shoulder
- Neck
- Front arm
- Forearm

Third Day

Warm-Up

Cardio
Walk, jog, or ride a bicycle 15 to 30 minutes as described in the cardio programs detailed in Chapter 5.

Strength Training
Shoot for 3 sets of 10 to 15 reps.
- Squat
- Leg extension
- Leg curl
- Modified deadlift
- Lunge
- Standing calf press
- Sitting calf press
- Swing throw
- Front throw
- Crunch (3 sets of 15 to 25)
- Hip tilt (3 sets of 15 to 25)

Stretching
- Low back
- Glutes
- Hips
- Front thighs
- Back thighs
- Calves

Advanced (Four Times Per Week)

This program is for those who have spent some time in a gym and know their way around a bit more. Use 4 sets per exercise here with enough weight that you may only be able to get 7 or 8 reps on the final set. Also, you can experiment with some subtle changes like doing push-downs with a straight bar instead of a curved bar and changing arm angles on other exercises to give some variation to the challenges you present to your muscles. Also, consider trying some supersets, in which you do 1 set of two different exercises immediately after each other. For instance, you might do 10 incline dumbbell press reps and immediately follow with 10 sitting dumbbell press reps.

Warm-Up

Cardio
Same as the standard workout, but add a second day of high-intensity interval training.

First Day

Strength Training
- Bench press
- Incline dumbbell press
- Push-up
- Lying triceps press
- Cable push-down
- Dip
- Swing throw
- Front throw

Stretching
Do all the stretches detailed at the end of Chapter 4.

Second Day

Strength Training
- Lat pull (wide grip)
- Lat pull (narrow grip)

- Seated row
- Dumbbell row
- Back extension
- Sitting dumbbell curl
- Standing bar curl
- Swing throw
- Front throw

Stretching
Do all the stretches detailed at the end of Chapter 4.

Third Day

Strength Training
- Sitting dumbbell press
- Lateral raise
- Dumbbell row
- All medicine ball throws
- Crunch (4 sets of 25 each)
- Hip tilt (4 sets of 25 each)

Stretching
Do all the stretches detailed at the end of Chapter 4.

Fourth Day

Strength Training
- Squat
- Leg extension
- Leg curl
- Modified deadlift
- Lunge
- Standing calf press
- Sitting calf press

Stretching
Do all the stretches detailed at the end of Chapter 4.

Juniors and Seniors

Golfers come in every shape and size and from every walk of life, but there are at least two subgroups that deserve special attention when it comes to golf fitness—young, still-developing golfers who have a whole life of swings ahead of them and more "experienced" players who continue to wring pleasure from the game even as their bodies seem less willing to cooperate. This chapter will take a look at the special needs of each of these groups, so that players both old and new to the game can maximize their golfing potential.

Juniors

We all know that Tiger Woods started playing golf when he was three years old. But Michael Jordan didn't play high school basketball until his junior year, the same age Lawrence Taylor started playing football. You don't have to have hit your first shot in diapers to become a great golfer. By the same token, you shouldn't start a hardcore fitness regimen until you're in your early to mid-teens and your body is well on the way to physical maturity.

Current research suggests that preadolescents can gain strength and flexibility from working out, but there are also concerns about injuring or overstressing still-developing bones and joints. And while physical training can help little kids burn calories and develop muscle control and coordination, they don't really gain cardiovascular benefits from exercise and they can't exhaust heat as well as adults, which means they're more prone to heat stress. So there's no rush. The main thing for young kids to remember when doing any exercise is to have fun.

But by the time you reach your early teens—or, more specifically, puberty—you can start to think about a fitness plan to enhance your sports performance, regardless of what sport or sports you play. You should still be playing more than one at this point, because specializing in one sport too early can lead to burnout and even inhibit your overall athletic development by limiting your training.

For young golfers, then, the first step is to decide to start working out. If it's something pushed from the outside and not part of a strong internal motivation, it won't do any good. Not working out at this point in your golf career doesn't mean you have to stop playing golf or that you'll never be a great player; it just means you haven't reached that next level of commitment to your game, which is fine.

But once you make the decision to start working out, your next step, if you haven't already taken it, should be golf lessons. Nothing will cause you more heartache or lead to more injuries than poor technique. With still-developing bodies, injury prevention is the first priority, both on the driving range and in the weight room. The concern is that even minor injuries can get more serious over time if not treated properly and could eventually harm growth areas, leading to developmental problems. So see a qualified professional and learn how to swing the club properly, and make sure you're playing with clubs that are the right size and weight. Dad's leftovers might be economically preferable, but they could hurt your development and your body.

Your workouts will contain the same types of exercises and training as those for adults, but with a number of extra cautions and points of technique. First, as always, get a physical from your doctor before starting, and continue seeing your doctor regularly so he or she can note any emerging concerns.

Then make sure you know how to use the equipment. Even if you're working out at home, make an appointment with a personal trainer who can teach you the correct and safe way to use the equipment and perform the exercises. Most trainers are happy to come to your house, or they can get you a one-day pass to a gym where they regularly work.

When you meet with the trainer, ask how to precisely take your heart rate, which is critical to effective cardiovascular training. And find out how to provide a spot for someone who's using the various equipment, because ideally you'll have a training partner whom you'll spot and who will spot you. Spotting is not only a major safety consideration while working out, but having a partner makes it easier to stick with a program. On days you don't feel up to it, a partner can motivate you if for no other reason than you're supposed to meet him.

And remember that a spotter's there to do more than just help you out if you can't complete a set. She should know the right way to do the exercises and help you maintain proper form. Proper form includes performing the movement slowly, maintaining correct posture, and working through the full range of motion. Also, don't hold your breath or arch your back. One of the best ways to injure yourself is to perform the exercise incorrectly—especially for a golfer, to whom precise movements should be of utmost importance and carried through in everything.

Younger athletes should also avoid "working through" injury or pain, the practice of ignoring minor aches and pains in order to continue working out. While this has less potential downside for adults when done properly and under the right circumstances, it can be much more harmful to those whose bodies are still growing. If you have some sort of injury or pain, take a few days off until it heals or stops hurting. If the symptoms persist, seek medical attention.

By the same token, you should be careful not to overtrain by pushing too hard or not giving your body ample recovery time. Even more than adults, adolescents need to give their muscles time to rebuild between workouts. In fact, it's wise to try to get more sleep when you're in a training program. For these reasons it's generally recommended that early teens work out no more than three times a week for no more than an hour (including cardiovascular training) and perform exercises in 3 sets of 10. If you can't do 10 repetitions, you have too much weight. When you're ready to add weight, do it in small (three- to five-pound) increments.

And don't forget to warm up, cool down, and stretch while you're working out. For a golfer and someone who's still growing, flexibility is a top priority. You don't want your muscle development to inhibit your ability to make a full swing.

Eat a good balanced diet (not too high in protein); make sure to drink plenty of fluids before, during, and after a workout; and try to eat a high-protein snack after you train.

Workout Program: Juniors (Three Times Per Week)

This program is for early to mid-teens who've started maturing physically. Make sure to keep it fun. For instance, consider a little on-course wagering, but instead of betting money, bet push-ups. Every hole you lose you do 10 push-ups—right on the spot. Win the hole and your buddies are the ones dropping and drooling. Also, young golfers should try doing extra medicine ball throws from the weak side to develop balance.

Warm-Up

Cardio
Walk, jog, or ride a bicycle 15 to 30 minutes as described in the cardio programs detailed in Chapter 5.

Strength Training
Shoot for 3 sets of 10 to 15 reps.
- Push-up
- Dip
- Crunch
- Hip tilt
- Back extension

- Squat (with medicine ball)
- Lunge (with medicine ball)
- Standing calf press (no weight)
- Squeeze a tennis ball (for forearms)
- All the medicine ball throws

Stretching

Do all the stretches detailed at the end of Chapter 4.

Seniors

In 2003 Arnold Palmer played in his forty-ninth straight Masters. At the tender age of seventy-three, the veteran of prostate cancer surgery faced unusually wet and difficult conditions on one of the hardest golf courses in the world. He shot an eighty-three. The point of this story? You should not only be able to enjoy golf late in life, there's no reason you can't continue to play well.

The key, of course, is keeping your body up to the effort. More than anyone, the senior golfer stands to gain from a regular workout program, not just on the course but in all aspects of life. As previously stated, lifting weights and resistance training can minimize and in some cases even reverse the effects of losses in bone density and muscle mass. Overall training, including cardiovascular workouts, can bolster the immune system and reduce the risk of certain types of cancer, high blood pressure, diabetes, and osteoporosis.

This is not to say that you'll be as strong and flexible as you were at twenty, but if you're currently physically inactive you can turn the clock back quite a bit by increasing physical activity. If you're already fairly active, then you can start to make greater long-term improvements to your health and your golf game. In addition, working out can help you maintain a healthy weight or even lose weight, another achievement that comes with a long list of health benefits.

Consult a doctor before starting any exercise program and see a physical fitness expert about which exercises to do and how to do them. This is particularly important for anyone with a heart condition, diabetes, high blood pressure, bone or joint problems, or asthma.

Arnold Palmer (Photo courtesy of Arnold Palmer Enterprises)

Beyond that, inactive seniors should set up a program that gradually builds to at least thirty minutes of moderately intense exercise. Remember, though, it doesn't have to be thirty minutes straight, especially at the beginning. Three ten-minute sessions will do the trick. You can even start by turning the fairly mundane activities of everyday life into opportunities to get in better shape. During the day, walk in place a little while talking on the phone or do some housework or yardwork. When you go to the store don't hunt for the closest spot. Park farther away and enjoy the walk.

Whenever you work out remember to warm up first and begin slowly, gradually building intensity. Don't increase the intensity or duration of any workout by more than 10 percent in a week. Once you get your legs, or if you're already in reasonably good condition, consider a varied fitness regimen that takes the whole body into account. It should include at least four types of exercises:

- Cardiovascular training, which increases the heart rate and breathing for extended periods of time, improving not just stamina but the overall health of the heart, lungs, and circulatory system
- Strength or resistance training to get stronger and even increase muscle mass and bone density
- Balance exercises, which help prevent falls and maintain overall coordination
- Stretching to enhance flexibility and to help reduce the everyday stress

At all points along the way, stop exercising if anything starts to hurt (beyond a little minor muscle soreness) or if breathing becomes so difficult that you can't carry on a conversation. If something hurts, work around the pain, not through it; and if your workout is taking your breath away, reduce the intensity. Don't forget to drink water before, during, and after exercise, and make sure to wear the right shoes—ones that fit properly and offer adequate support and stability.

Consider a few things that make it easier to start and stick with a program. For starters, find a situation that works for you. Some like group activities; others like to work alone. Maybe you prefer swimming or in-pool classes or a more casual mall-walking appointment. Try different approaches; just be sure to find one you like and stick with it.

Find someone to train with, if possible—a walking buddy or a personal trainer keeps you motivated and helps build the ongoing social connections that are a key part of maintaining good health. Many gyms and community centers offer a wide array of exercise classes meant to suit virtually anyone's needs and interests. They're a great way to get in shape and pump up your social life as well.

Another good strategy is to set goals. They can be short-term or long-term (preferably both) but they should be achievable. Some can be far-off dreams, like running a mile or shooting 80, but most should be things that you know you can do, which gives you a sense of accomplishment and encourages you to stick with it. Even if it's something as simple as saying, "I'm going to go to the gym at least three days a week," that's an important goal and you should feel good about achieving it.

Workout Program: Seniors (Three Times Per Week)

The possibility of injury is greater for seniors, especially those who had been previously sedentary. The key is to start slowly, progress gradually, and seek assistance to make sure you're performing the exercises and stretches properly. On all the exercises try extra hard to maintain proper technique and don't go farther than is comfortable. If you're doing squats or lunges and you can go down only a few inches, then that's what you should do. And if anything hurts, don't do it.

Cardio
Walk or ride a bicycle 15 to 30 minutes as described in the cardio programs detailed in Chapter 5.

Strength Training
Shoot for 3 sets of 12 to 20 reps.
- Medicine ball squat
- Medicine ball lunge
- Crunch
- Hip tilt
- All the medicine ball throws

Stretching
Do all the stretches detailed at the end of Chapter 4.

The Long Ball

The long drive is golf's version of the slam dunk or home run. Its combination of power and majesty captures the imagination and incites in everyone who picks up a club a desire to simply crush the ball and watch it sail off endlessly toward the horizon. No matter how far you can hit the ball, you always want to hit it farther, as if another ten or fifteen yards off the tee would solve all your problems. Well, it probably won't hurt.

As you might suspect, working out so that you become stronger and more flexible can help you hit it far, but you have to know which muscle groups to focus on and how to use them. No doubt an increased emphasis on fitness is part of the reason golf balls are flying farther than ever. But other factors are at work as well.

First and foremost is the equipment. Titanium heads with super-thin faces, longer clubs, and better shafts have all had an impact, but by far the biggest factor in increasing driving length statistics is the ball. Today's golf balls simply fly farther with more spin and control characteristics than balls of even five years ago, never mind ten or twenty years ago. They fly so far, in fact, that the rule-making organizations of golf are considering a special limited-flight tournament ball that professionals would have to use in competition. Such balls would help level the playing field and save golf courses from expensive and sometimes impossible renovations in order to keep from being rendered obsolete by today's long hitters. Par 72 doesn't have much meaning when the whole field can reach every par 5 in two shots and drive within wedge distance of every par 4.

Of course, those of you just trying to post a decent score can and should take advantage of all the advanced equipment you can get. For you, the bigger issue, and something you need to focus on in order to hit the ball longer, is technique.

The biggest, strongest guy in the world can't hit the ball very far without the proper technique. At the same time, good technique allows golfers with relatively small physiques, like Charles Howell III and Sergio Garcia, to regularly uncork 300-yard drives. Just as important, their technique helps them control the shot, because there's no use hitting the ball a mile if you can't keep it in play with some consistency.

Because this is not an instruction book, we're not going to get into the details of how technique promotes distance. But in order to discuss how fitness promotes distance we need to at least have some common understanding about technique. For that reason we've highlighted four elements of the swing that are key when you're trying to hit it long.

First, think wide. At the start of the backswing and all the way to the top, try to keep your hands as far away from your body as possible. This promotes what golf instructors like to call *width*, which naturally helps you get more clubhead speed. Imagine a six-foot-long rope with two knots tied in it, one at the end and one in the middle. If you pick that rope up and twirl it over your head like a lasso, the knot at the end, the one that's farther from the center of the circle, is going to be moving faster than the knot in the middle, which is only half as far away. If you want the clubhead to move faster, keep it as far away from the center of your swing as possible.

Next, turn your shoulders. Getting a full shoulder turn makes your swing longer, which means it has more time to build speed and power before impact. In fact, the offset between your hips and shoulders creates the noticeable tension in your body at the top of the backswing, and converting that tension into torque creates power.

Third, drive with your legs. Think of your golf swing as cracking a whip. The point at which you have the club over your head is equivalent to the moment you've got that whip loaded up over your head. What starts the swing motion forward is driving off the ground with your feet. The energy of that initial drive is what moves up through your body and cracks that club through the ball. This is the same reason a baseball pitcher who throws a ninety-five-mile-per-hour fastball has not just a strong arm, but strong legs. Leg drive is what allows a pitcher to throw the ball so hard, and it's what allows golfers to hit it far.

Finally, swing through the ball. If you really want to hit for distance, the object of your swing should not be the ball. You shouldn't "hit" the ball. What you should try to do is throw the clubhead at the target, as if the clubhead could slide off the end of the club during follow-through and fly at the spot you're aiming for. The ball should be nothing more than a little something that gets in your way as you swing at your real objective, which is the target.

So how does working out help you achieve these four things? Some of the ways are obvious and some are not. Getting good width on your swing requires flexibility, because if you can't reach those spots way above your head, you can't get a golf club up there. At the same time it requires more shoulder, arm, and hand strength, because the farther that club gets from your body, the harder it is to control.

Greater shoulder turn also requires greater flexibility throughout the hips and upper body, but beyond that it requires greater strength through the same region. In order to really get that great rotational pull, you need strength throughout the core muscles of the body and in the side of your back (the lats) and your chest (the pecs).

Greater leg strength helps create the extra drive you need, but it does more than that. The legs are your base, and whether you're putting, hitting a five iron, or driving, you can't do anything without a strong, solid base. As you take these steps to make your swing longer and wider and therefore increase your clubhead speed, your base needs to be even stronger to keep you stable through the extra effort.

This emphasizes once again the need for balance—not only in the sense of keeping your balance while making a big, smooth swing through the ball, but in the sense of body and muscle balance. Having that muscular equilibrium will not only allow you to be steady and relaxed through the swing, which is the key to really ripping it, but also let you create controlled movement at high speed. Let's not forget that control is a major part of this. Just swinging hard isn't the answer. If you can't hit the ball far and straight, you're better off hitting short.

Workout Program: The Long Ball

This program is for those who want to hit it farther. Anyone doing the one-, two-, three-, or four-day workouts should add one set of each of the following.

- Squats (10 to 15 reps)
- Lunges (10 to 15 reps)
- Crunches (15 to 25 reps)
- Hip tilts (15 to 25 reps)
- Swing throws (10 to 15 reps)
- Front throws (10 to 15 reps)

Nutrition

Now comes the hard part: eating. Everyone loves to do it, but it gets a lot of us in trouble. Most people could afford to lose at least a few pounds, and even the laudably trim could probably do well by eating a little better. After all, your eating habits can influence your risk of developing heart disease, cancer, stroke, diabetes, osteoporosis, and high blood pressure. Certainly, eating right is a major part of any fitness regimen. Beyond that, knowing what, when, and how to eat can actually help your golf game.

Eating for Good Health

You can't understand the basics of nutrition without first understanding a few things about how the body works. Food contains millions of tiny chemicals we commonly refer to as *nutrients*. The body is made up of millions of tiny units we refer to as *cells*. These cells process the nutrients in order to carry out everyday bodily functions, provide us with energy, and build and repair body tissue. As we know from an earlier chapter, building and repairing body tissue is the basis of any successful workout routine, so you can see right away how important good nutrition is to effective workouts.

The problem is that all nutrients are not created equal. Generally, they're broken down into three main groups, with water as a fourth. Within the groups there are subdivisions that make the matter seem more complex, although it's really not that hard to understand once you become familiar with the terms.

First there are the *carbohydrates*, the most common of the nutrients and the body's main supply of energy, which the body stores as calories. The carbohydrate category is subdivided into *complex carbohydrates* and *simple carbohydrates*. Simple carbs—fruits, milk, certain vegetables, sugars—go directly into the bloodstream and provide a quick burst of energy. For the most part you want to pass on the simple carbs, although if you must have them go for the milk and fruits, as these at least offer something in the way of vitamins and minerals. The sugars, including everything from honey to candy to apple juice, do nothing but offer empty calories that give an initial jolt to your system. In fact, any of those calories you don't immediately burn off get converted to fat for storage.

That's why you're better off fashioning your diet out of a higher percentage of complex carbs, things like whole-grain bread, cereal, and pasta; rice; vegetables; and legumes. It takes the body longer to break down these foods, which means they supply a slower, steadier stream of energy over a longer period of time, increasing the likelihood that you'll burn them off and decreasing the chance they'll end up getting stored as fat. In addition, they offer far more in the way of vitamins and minerals, which the body also needs to function properly.

After the carbs come the *proteins*, which can also serve as a source of calories for the body to burn but are really there to serve more important functions. For starters, they form enzymes that play crucial roles in various body functions. And, most important to those looking to build strength and muscle, proteins form the building blocks of new and repaired tissue. So if you want to get stronger, look to protein-rich foods like beef, poultry, fish, dairy products, vegetables, legumes, and nuts.

Be aware, though, that at least some of those items that are high in protein—certain cuts of beef and dairy products—are also high in one final group of nutrients that are not so good for you: *fats*. Fat is not all bad; it supports organs and cells, insulates, allows the absorption of certain vitamins, and provides fatty acids that are essential to the body. It also provides the primary source of calories once all the carbs are burned up.

But it is also the source of artery-clogging cholesterol, excess body fat, and obesity, all of which have a long list of unhealthy side effects. The trick is to remember that there are different kinds of fat. The "good" fats are those found in plant-based products, such as olive, nut, and canola oils and vegetable oils (corn, sunflower, and safflower, for example). The "bad" fats are those that come from animal sources, such as meats, dairy products, and poultry skin, and from chemically altered fats, such as most shortenings and anything partially hydrogenated. There are exceptions; for example, certain fish fats are good and palm oil is bad.

Knowing all that, the idea for general health is to shoot for a diet that draws about 55 percent of its calories from carbohydrates, 30 percent from fat, and 15 percent from protein. The nutritional and caloric information for all store-bought food is available right on the label, including total calories, calories from fat, protein, carbohydrates, and sugars. Be aware, though, that the information reflects single servings and the container usually holds more than one serving. For instance, a 16-ounce bottle of juice will show that it has 100 calories per serving. But if you look closely you'll see it says there are two servings per container, which means that 16-ounce bottle has 200 calories. For restaurant food, you can find good estimates of nutritional information on any one of a number of great websites. Try searching for "calorie calculator" or "calorie estimator."

The majority of your carbohydrates should be complex and the majority of the fats should be "good." Weightlifters, athletes, and those seeking improved fitness often tweak those percentages, upping the protein portion to anywhere from 20 to 40 percent and cutting down on both carbs and fat. Such diets can be effective for both losing weight and building muscle—and are currently very popular—but anyone considering such a mix should be aware that some experts believe there are health risks associated with high protein consumption over long periods.

Almost as important as eating good foods is eating a wide variety of foods. If you eat the same three healthy meals over and over, your body will only get the vitamins and minerals contained within those foods. In order to get the variety of vitamins and minerals you need, you must eat different foods. So shoot not just for veggies and meats and whole grains, but a wide assortment of each.

In addition, you should try to eat most of your carbs earlier in the day so you have a better chance of burning them off before you settle in for the night. And try to eat five or six small meals a day, each about three hours apart, instead of three big ones. Your body is extremely good at protecting against starvation, so when it goes too long without food it automatically kicks in its survival tactics and stores as many calories as it can as fat. Giving it a steady supply of slow-burning fuel will keep it from going into starvation mode and therefore stoke up your metabolism, making your body more efficient.

Last, don't forget water. It makes up about 55 percent of your body weight and performs a number of essential functions: regulating body temperature, carrying nutrients and oxygen to the cells, cleansing your system, and cushioning your joints. In general, experts recommend drinking about eight glasses, or 64 ounces a day.

Eating to Lose Weight

Changing your eating habits and starting an exercise program should cause you to lose some weight. But if you're already eating pretty well, or if you're not willing to make the wholesale changes required for a healthy diet, there are still things you can do to shed a few pounds.

First, avoid the fad diets. While they can help you lose a lot of weight quickly, they're almost impossible to stay on, and when you falter you usually gain back the weight you lost, plus some, almost as quickly. The better bet, and an easier solution, is to make some relatively small and painless changes to your eating habits and lifestyle. With almost no suffering you can lose one to two pounds per week.

The Numbers Racket

To calculate how many calories you should consume per day to lose weight, use the following formula.

Current weight $\times$ 13 $\times$ 0.7 = target calories (if you already work out three times a week, multiply by 15 instead of 13)

To calculate how many grams of fat you can consume per day to lose weight, use the following formula.

Desired weight $\times$ 0.45 = fat grams/day

To determine whether you need to lose weight, calculate your body mass index (BMI). A score of 25 or more is considered overweight.

Your weight $\div$ 2.2 = A

Your height in inches $\div$ 39 = Y

Y $\times$ Y = B

A $\div$ B = BMI

A pound of fat equals about 3,500 calories, so in order to lose a pound a week you need to cut about 500 calories a day; for two pounds, about 1,000 a day. You can achieve that by any combination of reducing your intake and increasing the number of calories you burn. A good place to start is by writing down everything you eat for two or three days in a row. Then examine the findings and look for places where you can make some changes.

Drinks are a great place to start. A typical soft drink has anywhere from 130 to 200 calories. Switch to water or a diet version and you've got zero. Beer has anywhere from 150 to 400 calories per bottle. Try drinking one fewer or switching to lite and you can cut a few hundred more. Drinking skim milk instead of whole saves 100 calories.

Look for similar calorie-saving replacement foods. Instead of a bacon, egg, and cheese sandwich for breakfast, try a bagel and lose about 200 calories. How about popcorn instead of potato chips? Another 100 or so. Instead of a cheeseburger, go for the turkey cheeseburger, or just drop the cheese. Consider asking for a salad instead of french fries. Again, most of the nutritional and calorie information for almost any meal is available online with just a little checking.

If you decide one day you really have to have some ice cream, that's OK—just know you have to make up for it somewhere else.

And think about portion sizes, too. Don't just sit down with a plate of pasta or a bag of popcorn. Look at the serving size and put that much on the plate or into a bowl. And once you've had your share, put it away, along with all the other tempting goodies, before you wind up packing it away.

Dieting Tips

- Eat five or six small meals a day to maintain blood sugar levels and avoid feeling hungry.
- If you eat more whole grains and vegetables, you'll have less room for the bad stuff.
- Sauces and beverages are often an unsuspected source of anywhere from 70 to 200 calories.
- Just because something is fat free or lite doesn't mean it's low in calories.
- Häagen-Dazs comes in those nice little containers, but calorie information is per serving, not per package.

Eating on the Course

For the most part you should try not to eat too much right before playing or while you're out on the course. A full stomach causes your body to divert its attention and blood flow to your digestive system instead of to the muscles you need to play golf. Essentially, you're forcing your body to fight with itself, especially if you eat greasy, heavy foods that take a lot of effort to digest, exactly the kind of stuff you find in many clubhouses and halfway carts.

A better idea is to eat well before you play and carry a few well-chosen snacks along with you. Try a banana or an apple, or maybe a few granola bars. Don't be afraid to eat more than one snack spaced out over the course of a round. Such complex carbohydrates will give you plenty of healthy, slow-burning fuel to get you through the round without fatigue.

Drink plenty of water, too. In fact, if you wait until you feel thirsty you've probably waited to long. Thirst is a sign that your body is already running short of fluids. You want to replenish before that happens. If it's not obvious, you should drink more on hot days; and if it's especially hot and you're sweating a lot, you should consider a sports drink, which will not only keep you hydrated but will replace your body's electrolytes.

Injuries

The best way to treat a golf injury is to not get one in the first place. There are a couple of simple things you can do to help keep yourself from getting hurt. The first three rules of golf injury prevention are take a lesson, take a lesson, and take a lesson. The majority of a golfer's aches and pains can be traced back to some imperfection in the swing that puts strain on one or more parts of the body and over time causes a problem that leads to pain. Making sure you have a smooth swing through the proper arc helps alleviate a lot of those strains without costing you anything in distance or accuracy—in fact, taking a few lessons should help every aspect of your game.

Beyond that, almost every medical and fitness expert recommends strength training, stretching, and proper warm-up as the best ways to prevent injury. Lucky for you (and not by coincidence), those are all things I've focused on in this book and that should be a part of your new routine. As I've already discussed, a lack of muscle balance alone can lead to injury, but it's a two-way street: an injury can also cause a muscle imbalance. Either way, getting started on a fitness routine will help by correcting those imbalances before they hurt you and by reducing the risk of injury that can lead to an imbalance.

Still, even the best-trained golfers can get hurt. In the last few years alone two of my clients have missed time with injury. Jesper Parnevik suffered a tear in the tissue around his hip that required surgery, a classic overuse injury. And Vijay Singh pulled a muscle in his rib cage while hitting balls, an example of a one-time trauma injury. Even the great Tiger missed a few months after having surgery on a non-golf-related injury to his knee.

After doing everything you can to prevent injuries, the next step is learning how to recognize them and knowing what to do about them when they pop up. The first rule with any physical activity is to stop if it hurts. You have to use your own judgment to some degree in deciding whether you're just experiencing the kind of soreness you can play through or it's something more serious. If it hurts enough to keep you from swinging the way you normally do, that's probably a pretty good sign that it's time to put the club down.

Take a week or two off, trying to give the injured area complete rest. Then take a few practice swings. If you're pain free, start hitting some balls—nice, easy short irons at first, then work your way up. Go home and sleep on it. If you're still pain free the next day, go ahead and try playing. If the pain resurfaces at any point in the process, stop and consult a professional. Take heart, though; most golf injuries are not serious and can be fixed with the most basic sports medicine treatments—that is rest, immobilization, ice or heat, anti-inflammatory drugs, and stretching and strengthening. The exact combination of these steps should be determined by a doctor.

It's worth taking time to single out and dissect the specific injuries that most often affect golfers because often you can take specific steps to prevent them, recognize them, and eliminate them. These areas of common injury include the back, shoulder, elbow, and wrist.

It should come as no surprise to anyone who's ever swung a golf club that the most frequent area of pain is the lower back. The golf swing is a rather unnatural motion, and the twisting it requires puts a lot of strain on the lower back—especially if you have poor posture and muscle balance. Studies have shown that the lower spine encounters a load about eight times the golfer's body weight during the swing and that amateur golfers, on average, actually subject their back to more strain than professionals. That's because pros have a more refined swing that provides distance through proper mechanics rather than through just swinging hard.

So although most back injuries are minor muscle strains that will heal quickly if treated properly, it is nevertheless possible to rupture a disc or even get a compression fracture of the vertebrae from playing golf. To avoid injury, you can take some steps to relieve the pressure on your lower back.

Try shortening your backswing to cut down on the difference between your hip and shoulder turn. Yes, this will probably cause you to lose some distance, but you can make that up by learning to swing the club more efficiently and working out so you have more strength. Second, try finishing your swing by stopping in a nearly vertical position instead of flexing your back into a curve. To do this, you really have to transfer that weight onto the front foot, which makes for a better swing anyway.

Last, try bending at the knees instead of the waist to tee your ball and pluck it out of the hole. The excessive bending you do during the course of a round puts additional strain on your lower back. If you have consistent lower back pain you might even consider getting one of those little suction cups you can stick on the butt end of your putter so you don't have to bend over to pick up the ball. They're not cool, but they serve a purpose.

After a bad back, the next most common injury is golfer's elbow, an inflammation of the tendons on the inside of the elbow, although it sometimes occurs on the outside. It comes from either overrotating your wrists throughout the swing instead of just before and just after contact, gripping the club too tightly, or the repetitive impact of hitting both the ball and the ground. Not to be redundant, but improving your swing so you don't hit the ground as much, making purer contact so you don't get as much vibration back up through the club, learning a proper grip, and avoiding overrotating your wrists should prevent this one from appearing.

If it does occur, a simple forearm brace, the kind used for tennis elbow, usually relieves the pain by taking the pressure off the tendons in question. Your equipment can help, too. Larger grips cut down on wrist rotation and are easier to hold, and a club with a larger sweet spot and graphite shaft reduces the vibration feedback.

Next up is shoulder pain. You can hurt either shoulder playing golf, but usually it's the front shoulder that starts to ache. And why not? It must work through an incredible range of motion during the swing and flex in several directions. The stress can cause any number of minor problems, from forms of tendinitis to impingement syndrome to rotator cuff tears. In any of these cases the best way to keep the shoulder healthy is to make sure your rotator cuff muscles are strong (the medicine ball throws in my programs are a great way to strengthen them) and that your shoulders are well stretched and warmed up before play. After that, you can consider cutting down on your backswing—which also relieves that back strain—to ease the burden on your shoulders.

Last are the hands and wrists, which, like the elbow, must absorb a lot of the feedback from the club upon impact and must rotate quickly during the swing. Both of these can cause injuries to tendons and muscles in the hand, as can snapping your wrists too early in the swing. As with golfer's elbow, some equipment changes and better form can help. So can building up the muscles in the wrists and forearms.

Injuries happen, even in golf. But with good swing mechanics and a proper training regimen you can certainly cut down on their frequency and severity. It's worth the effort because golf is a game you can play well your whole life as long as you keep yourself reasonably prepared.

Mental Balance

I've talked a lot in this book about muscle balance because I truly believe it's the key to improved physical performance in almost everything you do. It allows the bones, muscles, tendons, and ligaments to interact the way they were meant to and adds a level of power, flexibility, and grace to everything you do. But the benefits of muscle balance go beyond the purely physical. By promoting good posture, muscle balance actually gets into the psychological and physiological realms of performance as well.

Golf may be a refined game with a courtly tradition of honor and sportsmanship, but that doesn't mean it's beyond the laws of the jungle. I remember once watching a nature show in which two gorillas were fighting for control of the group. The two would charge each other and partake in brief but fierce physical exchanges, then separate and stare each other down, screaming, gesturing, and feinting before the next battle.

The actual fighting showed no sign of a winner, with each animal throwing himself fully into the fray and attacking the other with abandon. But during the periods leading up to the clashes, I noticed that one of them stood up a little taller, puffed his chest out more, and was generally more aggressive. The other slouched a little and kept his head down. It wasn't much of a difference, nothing obvious or overt, just a slight variation in body posture that told the whole story. Sure enough, the tall, aggressive one prevailed over his worthy but a little less assertive opponent.

I thought this little scene was particularly applicable to a sport like golf, where often the gorilla you're competing against is yourself. When you allow yourself to get down, either before hitting a difficult shot or after a bad one, you're giving in to the posture of self-defeat. When you see golfers on the course with slumped shoulders and heads down, you can bet that they just hit a bad shot and they're about to hit another one. If for no other reason than good golf requires good posture, letting yourself sag is a bad idea.

This is something that the world's best golfer is particularly good at. Have you ever seen a golfer who was more fit and upright and athletic looking than Tiger? He doesn't just walk around out there—he strides, chin up, chest out, with purpose and determination. Even when he hits a bad shot, he may get mad, slam his club, or rip off his glove, but then he forgets it and gets right back into his posture and his rhythm.

By not getting down physically, he prevents himself from getting down mentally, which keeps his game at a high level and sends a signal to his competitors that he's still not beaten. Golfers who get down and show signs of defeat both physically and mentally not only hurt their focus and decrease their chances of playing well, they subconsciously encourage their competitors or playing partners.

By almost forcing you to have good posture, muscle balance can help you win this psychological part of the game, too. In fact, when you have poor muscle balance and tone and you let yourself relax and just let your muscles hang, you often morph into some sort of C-shaped slump. But when you have proper muscle balance, a fully relaxed position is one in which you have almost perfect posture. Think of how nice it would feel to really relax all your muscles and still have perfect posture.

Good posture offers physiological benefits as well. When you stand upright with your shoulders back, it naturally opens up your chest and lungs. In such a position, you get more air into your lungs with each breath. This lets your body deliver more oxygenated blood to your muscles, making them work more efficiently. It also means you don't have to take as many breaths, which keeps you more relaxed and focused. In fact, taking faster, shorter breaths can kick in the body's natural defense mechanisms and trigger a whole series of chemical reactions in the brain that can make it harder to perform well.

For instance, such fight-or-flight responses can cause the release of adrenaline, that marvelous hormone that allows people to perform at accelerated levels—running faster, jumping higher, lifting cars off train tracks, and so on. Adrenaline is a godsend if you're playing football or trying to wage battle with an angry gorilla, but it's not so good if you're trying to hit a six-iron onto a small green from 165 yards out or attempting a downhill four-footer for par.

For golfers, it's better to stay relaxed and focused even after you make a great shot. You don't want to get too fired up—no fist pumping—because it can throw off the delicate mixture of heart rate, brain chemicals, and muscle control that allowed you to execute the shot in the first place.

What you need, of course, is balance—balance brought on by a good mental attitude, which is promoted by good posture, which comes from good muscle balance. It's a circle with no definitive starting and ending point that repeats over and over, and the best place to get on the track is at the gym.

This has been particularly important in my work with Vijay Singh. Despite all our efforts to build muscle balance and focus on staying positive, when things start going bad for Vijay—bad hole, a few bad shots—he tends to get into the old habit of hanging his head, which, as we know, only leads to a downward spiral. In order to counteract that, I have taught Vijay a few on-course rituals that promote balance.

The first involves rotating his wrists. (You may have seen him do this when watching him on TV and wondered what he was doing.) As he walks down the fairway Vijay will bend his arms at the elbow and extend his hands out in front of him. He then rotates his hands so his palms face the sky, then he pushes his elbows toward each other (as in 12.1 on page 138). The movement automatically forces him to roll his shoulders

12.1

back and expand his chest, improving his posture and therefore his mental outlook, and opening his lungs, allowing him to breathe more efficiently and stay relaxed.

The second is a rather simple pose that most people perform while warming up and then forget during the round. He simply grasps either end of a club and holds it behind his neck. This has the same effect of rolling back the shoulders and opening the chest. Taking the time to perform both of these little exercises on the course can have an impact on your focus, stamina, mental attitude, and, most important, your scorecard.

No matter what happens out there, remember, it's all about balance.

Index

A number followed by an *f* indicates a page with photos.